Using Multiliteracies *and* Multimodalities *to* Support Young Children's Learning

Education at SAGE

SAGE is a leading international publisher of journals, books, and electronic media for academic, educational, and professional markets.

Our education publishing includes:

- accessible and comprehensive texts for aspiring education professionals and practitioners looking to further their careers through continuing professional development

- inspirational advice and guidance for the classroom

- authoritative state of the art reference from the leading authors in the field

Find out more at: **www.sagepub.co.uk/education**

Marie Charles *and* Bill Boyle

Using Multiliteracies *and* Multimodalities *to* Support Young Children's Learning

SAGE

Los Angeles | London | New Delhi
Singapore | Washington DC

Los Angeles | London | New Delhi
Singapore | Washington DC

SAGE Publications Ltd
1 Oliver's Yard
55 City Road
London EC1Y 1SP

SAGE Publications Inc.
2455 Teller Road
Thousand Oaks, California 91320

SAGE Publications India Pvt Ltd
B 1/I 1 Mohan Cooperative Industrial Area
Mathura Road
New Delhi 110 044

SAGE Publications Asia-Pacific Pte Ltd
3 Church Street
#10-04 Samsung Hub
Singapore 049483

Editor: Marianne Lagrange
Editorial assistant: Rachael Plant
Production editor: Nicola Marshall
Copyeditor: Rose Campbell
Proofreader: Derek Markham
Indexer: Martin Hagreaves
Marketing manager: Catherine Slinn
Cover design: Wendy Scott
Typeset by: C&M Digitals (P) Ltd, Chennai, India
Printed in India at Replika Press Pvt Ltd

Library of Congress Control Number: 2013949538

British Library Cataloguing in Publication data

A catalogue record for this book is available from
the British Library

ISBN 978-1-4462-7334-0 (pbk)
ISBN 978-1-4462-7333-3

CONTENTS

LIST OF FIGURES

ABOUT THE AUTHORS

Marie Charles is a teacher, formative assessment researcher, consultant and author whose work demonstrates that she believes passionately in the learner (rather than measurement or grading) being at the centre of the education process – a belief that she carries into her classroom practice.

Professor Bill Boyle has until recently held the positions of chair of Educational Assessment and was Director of the Centre for Formative Assessment Studies (CFAS) in the Manchester Institute of Education at the University of Manchester, UK. CFAS is the oldest research centre (founded 1988) in the UK for supporting teachers, teacher trainers, schools and policy makers in using formative teaching, learning and assessment and is involved in supporting the development of formative assessment in the UK and in many countries around the globe. Professor Boyle and his co-author, Marie Charles, publish their research work in academic and practitioner journals, present at international conferences and workshops, and design and support developments in formative teaching, learning and assessment. Currently, they are working with colleagues in Pakistan, Russia, Armenia, Oman, Saudi Arabia and the USA on understanding and using formative strategies for more effective teaching and learning.

ACKNOWLEDGEMENTS

A special thank you to the individuals who believed in me; Jane Simpson, Sue Austin and Claude: A towering intellectual with great compassion who continues to influence my thinking.

And finally, a special thank you to McKelly Charles my dad, who taught me how to read at four years old and opened up to me the power of the printed word.

Marie Charles

INTRODUCTION

The principal theme of this book is an exploration of the process of developing young readers and writers through non-traditional means. To achieve this, we set out to demonstrate, illustrate and critique approaches to teaching through the use of multiliteracies (which we have exemplified through fiction, expository/ instructions, poetry, recount) and multimodalities (similarly through reading, writing, speaking, listening, performing, illustrating). Our aim was to present material which in the first instance would interest the reader/practitioner and hopefully provoke reflection and support the trainee/current teacher/researcher in understanding how to address and 'scaffold' the complex needs of a learner with depth and breadth. A commissioned report on behalf of the National Council for Curriculum and Assessment by Kennedy et al. (2012) built on a broad conceptualisation of the early work of Debes and recognises the importance of multiple modes and multiple representations in literacy. It also defines literacy from a semiotic position to include linguistic and non-linguistic forms of communication (Kennedy et al. 2012, p. 54).

We started from the premise (in both our teaching and our research) that as formative thinkers and practitioners we recognise the importance of formative assessment in the process of effective teaching and learning, and our aim is to build practitioners' understanding and capacity to use formative assessment in that process. Despite the strategies, myths and gimmicks that have been practised in its name, formative assessment is a simple concept. To borrow a quotation from Philippe Perrenoud: 'Any assessment that helps a pupil to learn and develop is formative' (1991, p. 80). It is important that teachers realise that an adjustment to their teaching is required, and that they know and understand how formative assessment helps the pupil to learn and how feedback from assessment supports that learning process.

In our understanding of the literature, a teacher's main role is to try to understand and support the learner on his/her journey to becoming an autonomous literate individual. Three key issues have emerged in our practical work and research – complexity, content knowledge and individual progression – and these three issues need application in the classroom situation to the 'real world' of the young learner seeking automaticity. For example, this can be achieved by introducing a multimodal aspect to the act of teaching, such as understanding how socio-dramatic play can support the emergent writer or how young communicators can support each other in narrative construction. Our philosophy is that teaching and learning demonstrate a mutually co-dependent and equal partnership between teacher and learner and that progress in learning depends to a large extent on the authentic involvement of the pupil in the learning process. Within the domain of writing development, we recognise and deconstruct for the reader the complexity of this process, that is, easing the cognitive load. This can be achieved by reducing the current unrealistic learning outcomes (expectations) caused by applying a 'one-size-fits-all' generalisation across a heterogeneous (classroom cohort) group to bring about a homogeneous learning outcome. How can these aims be achieved?

By supporting teachers to develop the understanding and use of various strategies (such as eliciting evidence, analysis and action) (Coffey et al., 2011) we intend that trainees/teachers will see the need to become more effective in identifying and using evidence to provide meaningful, relevant and progressive activities matched to individual learning interests and needs.

We saw the need for this book based on our classroom research (Boyle & Charles 2010a), which was based on observations and interviews with a representative national sample of primary school teachers and which produced evidence of limited training in, and understanding of, learning steps, learning trajectories (Heritage 2011) and progressions, especially within the domain of early literacy. We anticipated supporting formative teaching for deeper learning through the use in the book of concrete examples illustrated by case studies and step-by-step commentary. For example, the often quoted but mainly misunderstood concept of 'scaffolding' is addressed through modelling for the teacher on how to 'scaffold' a child struggling with the alphabet to write a decodable sentence independently through semiotics, pictures and other signs. Similarly, 'scaffolding' is a required strategy for the child who is regarded as able but requires support to develop more higher-order skills, and modelling of alternative experiences and strategies for deeper, richer learning is needed for the groups of children who 'get by' through disappearing into the 'acceptable level' category of the current measurement model.

We have tried to exemplify issues such as how to scaffold for the range of children's needs within the different language demands of the genres of poetry, narrative, expository texts, fantasy and recount. One example illustrates the developmental process for the child progressing from a first-person account and connecting back to her reading material and making those transferable connections to what she has written. The primacy of the processes of multimodality and multiliteracies in emerging literacy development are established. For example, themes such as the value to the learner of oral rehearsal leading to growth in aspects of literacy, are never de-contextualised and are always presented in an embedded, realistic way to the reader or learner. The book excludes a focus on product, outcomes, that is scores, levels, percentages, etc., but focuses on 'how' the child becomes a competent user of language, moving towards the goal of self-regulated learning and hence the journey to becoming a lifelong learner.

Children and their learning interests are at the centre of this book just as they have to be at the centre of all schools' language development programmes. The book focuses on the core pedagogical issues, such as the integration of teaching, learning and assessment; the crucial teacher-centred vs child-centred debate; didactic (transmission model) teaching vs formative (transactional learner-centred) teaching; homogeneity vs heterogeneity; and the pressures on learner-centred teaching of an accountability policy agenda.

We address major issues for successful language development and rich teaching pedagogy. These include the integration of modes of language development; immersion in types/modes of story, rhyme; teacher understanding of the importance of lessening the cognitive load and the implications of overloading 'working memory' for the learner, interest levels, motivation and commitment; relevance for the learner; in short, the importance of supporting the learner's affective domain and balancing the importance given to tests of cognition (understanding the triangulation and integration of cognitive, affective, conative domains on effective learning); and finally being sensitive to micro but vital developmental concerns for the young learner such as physicality (e.g. motor control, pencil grip, pacing, task completion, etc.).

We are singularly aware of the pressures teachers face in developing creativity and creative experiences for children while competing for space against current accountability and 'topical' political agendas for example phonics groups/testing, but we hope that the book will cause thinking, a period of reflection and possibly some changes in practice.

The principal theme of this book is an exploration of the process of developing young readers and writers through non-traditional means. We explore approaches to teaching through the use of multiliteracies (fiction, expository/instructions, poetry, recount) and multimodalities (reading, writing, speaking, listening, performing, illustrating). Our aim is to offer material which will support the reader in understanding how to 'scaffold' the complex needs of a learner. We believe that the teacher's main role is to try to understand and support the learner on his/her journey to becoming an autonomous literate individual.

The linking of teaching, learning and assessment as integrated concepts within a framework of multiliteracies and multimodalities

Let us look at definitions of multiliteracies and multimodalities (Kress 2003) and their relationships with formative teaching, learning and assessment. In a multimodal approach, communication occurs through different but synchronous modes: language, print, images, graphics, movement, gesture, music and sound (Kress 2003). In terms of multiliteracies: 'literacy pedagogy must account for the burgeoning variety of text forms associated with information and multi-media technologies and is a complex social, cultural and creative activity' (Nilsson 2010 p. 12) Formative assessment is a dynamic process of evidence elicitation, analysis and action which involves knowing what the learning goals are, eliciting evidence of pupil learning status relative to the goals, and taking action accordingly. Formative teachers are constantly attuned and responsive to pupils' learning progress.

Literacy theorists and researchers (Bruning & Horn 2000; Chapman & Turner 2003; Graves 1983; King-Sears 2005; Troia & Graham 2003) evidence that the child is central to this process; the learner is viewed as a unique learner. Basic but fundamental questions are: how can you develop an individual without a full understanding of that individual's starting point? Do I understand where the child is in his/her learning continuum? How can I move this child on? The Cox and Kingman reports of 1988 debated the 'distinction between what teachers need to know and what they should actually impart to their pupils' (Frater 2004, p. 78). Frater's case study of a struggling writer ('Dean') pinpoints the problem: 'the National Curriculum [has not] told me what is best actually to do; it has told me only where "Dean", with the teacher's help, needs to arrive' (p. 79). Frater (2004) finds that explicit instruction of English grammar is not appropriate. In theory, repetitive drilling which is often the mode of traditional grammar instruction, enables students to transfer the definitions memorised and the correct tenses circled on worksheets to their own writing. However, students usually fail when they are asked to transfer the rules of grammar recently learned from a unit to their own writing. Frater (2004) surveyed two schools in the United Kingdom (one at KS2 and the other at KS3/4) that were 'unusually effective in teaching writing' and conducted a case study of a low-achieving Year 7 writer (referred to as 'Dean'). In this case study Frater examines England's National Curriculum (specifically the National Strategies for Grammar for Writing, 2000 edition). Frater notes Dean's 'weak spellings, frequent failures with stops and caps, his faulty manuscript, distinctions between upper and lower case ...' (2004, p. 78). Additionally Frater (2004) finds that Dean's sentence patterns need attention and Dean makes little use of subordination, classifiers and modifiers. Based on his research, Frater (2004) argues that 'purposeful, text-level teaching, reading in particular, and the creation of real relationships, offer more secure ways of promoting progress in writing' (p. 78). After the National Literacy Strategy, DfEE's (2001) advice on developing early writing was not only outcomes oriented but was not supported by a solid research base (Dunsmuir & Blatchford 2004, p. 462).

Frater's (2004) case study illustrates that to achieve this 'movement' of the learner it is fundamental that the teacher understands the development phase model of the writing process which includes spelling and composition

(Education Department Western Australia 1997; Gentry 1982; Graves 1983). For example, Fresch's (2007) research, based on 355 teacher responses, highlighted the disparity between participants' current practices and theoretical beliefs about spelling instruction – for example, 72 per cent of teachers use one common spelling list for the entire class (p. 310). If teachers understood the developmental nature of the writing process then they would be implementing Flower's et al. (1986) assertion that 'the way people actually write is not adequately described by a model which suggests movement through discrete stages in a linear fashion' (in Yarrow & Topping 2001, p. 263). Instead, Flower's et al. (1986) metaphor of 'writers as switchboard operators juggling a number of different demands on their attention and various constraints on their behaviour' (in Yarrow & Topping 2001, p. 263) captures a learning model which although pedagogically sound has been made redundant by generations of teachers who follow the outcomes-oriented demands imposed by the National Strategies and Standards agenda. Current research (Alexander 2008; Boyle & Charles 2008, 2009; Burkard 2004; Eke & Lee 2004; Jolliffe 2004; Myhill 2006) evidences that the pedagogical model in classrooms today is based around one objective which does not seek to embrace the complexity that Flower describes and the individual learning requirements of a class. Graves (1983) analysed teachers and children at work as writers and in his work he described writing 'as a complex process rather than a single event, with great emphasis placed upon "rehearsal" for writing … day dreaming, sketching, doodling, making lists, outlining, reading, conversing, thinking about the product, ego boosting [i.e. thinking about the effect the writing will have on the readers, as well as the writer]' (p. 221). Both Flower (1989) and Graves (1983) understand and describe the necessary complexity of the writing process, a process which cannot be reduced to one objective because of the range of entry points of learners to the emergent writing process and the extent of conceptual understandings across the range. This provides further reinforcement of Martin, Segraves, Thacker and Young's (2005) adage that 'learning is a messy process' (p. 235). A major issue is to support the teacher who verbalises 'How do I help? What kind of help does the learner need?' For Sperling (1990):

> the teacher has to be involved with the [children] in small groups. Involvement in these small groups allows the teachers to ascertain where the [children] are in the writing ZPD [Zone of Proximal Development]. With the knowledge of the [children's] ZPD the teacher can provide the proper scaffolding to simplify the less needed cognitive tasks, allowing more cognitive energy for the writing strategy at hand. (In Vanderburg 2006, p. 389)

A four-month research study of 19 five- and six-year-olds was based on the development of writing workshops and mini lessons. It introduced the young learners to writing rough drafts, revising and editing through peer conferencing. Over the course of the project, the researchers reported increased motivation, enjoyment ('when are we going to publish another newspaper?'), more productive collaborative working and the development of qualitative evaluative questions by the learners. However, the limitations of small class size and no control group reduced the generalisability of the findings (Jasmine & Weiner 2007, p. 136). In contrast, the National Writing Project in England (1985–8) did not produce such rich outcomes despite its larger scale, better resourcing and multiplicity of published outcomes. Lambirth and Goouch (2006) in their critique of the project reported 'a strait-jacket of stylised conventional structure … imposed on the writing of a whole class so that individual learning by personal engagement with the experience is actually inhibited' (p. 147).

Martin et al.'s project (2005) involving three teachers and 63 first-grade pupils was guided by one research question: 'what do teachers and their [children] in first grade classrooms learn about writing when the writing process is added to the daily classroom instructional program?' (p. 240). The purpose of the research was to examine what the teachers and pupils learned about writing as the writing process was implemented in their classrooms throughout the school year. The teachers found that they had to examine their own beliefs and then to modify their pedagogy to accommodate the pupils' learning needs. Their findings included: 'first graders can and do want to write; learning is a messy process and empowerment is important for all' (Martin et al. 2005, p. 242). Specifically, one teacher 'discovered that the children in her classroom could use the different steps of the writing process … reflecting how the children's writing developed over time with guidance' (p. 242). These developments included 'becoming excited about using more colourful words … amazed because it had more detail' (we note that not using correct terminology could confuse children, for example when using labels such as 'colourful words'). And finally this study revealed that 'teachers can change their views about how and when pupils learn to write, but they [have] to be willing to make organisational and instructional changes' (p. 246). Most recently, in 2007 the DCSF recognised the importance of these 'organisational and instructional changes', that is, in this case a move away from the dominance of whole-class teaching. The DCSF introduced a guidance paper 'Improving writing with a focus on guided writing'. However, the main thrust of the guidance was identified as a means to focus on improving measured performance standards in writing, expressed in line 1 of the introduction as 'improving standards of writing at the end of Key Stage 2 is a national priority' (DCSF 2007a, p. 5). The guidance does, however, define and promote the use of guided writing as a supportive structure for developing writing for each individual, that is, 'the teacher is able to observe and respond to the needs of individuals within the group' (p. 6). However, if the development of the learner as an autonomous writer (Boyle & Charles 2009; Paris & Paris 2001; Zimmerman 2000) requires the pupil to be involved in the construction of their own learning, the guidance falls short in that it is didactic, highly structured and teacher-centred, that is, the 'teacher provides opening' (p. 22), 'the teacher constructs an imaginary situation' (p. 18), 'the teacher introduces the lesson objectives' (p. 32). The pupil is clearly seen in a fixed subordinate role, as evidenced by the guidance's instructions on setting up writing opportunities (p. 18), and the pedagogical model suggested echoes Alexander's (2004) 'closed recitation script'. The guidance (DCSF 2007a) fails to recognise the complexity and level of demand required for one to emerge as a proficient writer; it does not acknowledge the 'individualisation of the learning trajectory' (Perrenoud 1998, p. 98). The guidance rather follows the model of linear stepped progression to becoming a writer which was critiqued by Flower (1989) in her 'metaphor of the writer as a switchboard operator, juggling a number of different demands' (in Yarrow & Topping 2002, p. 263). Is this because the complexity inherent in pedagogy, as outlined by Flower (the requirement to 'juggle') and Perrenoud (the need to differentiate your teaching and learning programmes), may cause a 'perceived crisis in teachers' professional skills, routine and organisation' (Perrenoud 1998, p. 98). Has the summative agenda of the last twenty years reduced the capacity of the teacher so that 'juggling' and differentiating is now beyond them? In short, has the teacher been reduced to the technician who has been trained to deliver the whole-class menu but cannot diverge in his/her pedagogy to meet the learning needs of the individuals in their classrooms?

Outline of chapters

In Chapter 1 we illustrate how a young learner's writing needs were identified through evidence, elicitation and analysis (Coffey et al. 2011). The action agreed upon consequent to that analysis recognised that writing is a complex problem-solving activity which requires socio-dramatic play as the framework for structuring the child's development. Chapter 2 uses a case study to investigate the integration of major aspects of writing development such as collaboration, the importance of peer interactions through social learning and the fusion of illustrations, talk and writing to assist communication. The collaboration of the two girls as writers is tracked through four teaching interventions in which the girls chose the genre and writing aspects with equal status through this multimodal approach. Chapter 3's case study focuses on the reception and production of language and the judicious use of multimodal strategies (audio recorder, visual stills of fairytale scenes and props) and peer collaboration in supporting one boy's storytelling skills using the genre of fairytales. Chapter 4 focuses on a group of 'beginning readers' and the strategies being used by their teacher to deepen their understandings of the text being read aloud to the children and which the children read aloud themselves. The dominant strategy is the multimodal use of paintings and penned illustrations to create and author their own books. Chapter 5 details a case study in which a group of five children develop their 'Rain' poem through multimodal teaching strategies based around the socio-cognitive apprenticeship model of writing (Englert et al. 2006). The diverse range of outcomes expressed through their written poems illustrates how each individual child was able to self-regulate their impressions of the weather instead of replaying back to the teacher an imposed model 'from without' (Vygotsky 1978). The case study in Chapter 6 describes a strategy which supports the affective domain development of children, enabling them to feel good about engaging in the complex process of narrative construction. This process involved a deepening understanding of balancing transcription processes (with grapho-motor aspects) with the need to reduce the cognitive demand on working memory for the young writer (modelling/scribing). Chapter 7 focuses on a group of five-year-olds working initially from the story of the 'Owl Babies' and extending from that interest into non-fiction and the development of a reference book on owls. The children's illustrations initiated their text, facilitated by the teacher as scribe. Chapter 8 investigates the integration of genres (narrative to non-fiction) within a formative pedagogy). The case study demonstrates one teacher using guided group work as a potential strategy for a 'pedagogy of plenty' (Haberman 1991).

CHAPTER 1

USING SOCIO-DRAMATIC PLAY TO SUPPORT A BEGINNING WRITER

Introduction

Socio-dramatic play through the use of role play/scenarios and imaginary worlds has the capacity to support beginning writers. Christie (1991) argues that play can legitimately be used to accomplish learning objectives. Isenberg and Jacob (1983) provide a clear understanding of how symbolic play as a process of transforming an object, situation or event through the use of motor and verbal actions provides an important source for literacy development. (cited in Hall & Robinson 1998, p. 8)

This chapter illustrates how a very young boy's writing needs were identified through evidence elicitation and analysis (Coffey et al. 2011) – this action was agreed upon recognition that writing is a complex problem-solving activity and that complexity required socio-dramatic play as the framework for structuring the child's development. The chapter focuses on a case study of this young boy (aged 5) at a very early stage of his journey as a writer (see Figure 1.1: he is evidencing 'pre-alphabetic tendencies' [Gentry 1982]). Daniel is a talkative, communicative five-year-old who is very keen to tell the listener about the adventures of his dog. Daniel's baseline demonstrates his awareness that the production of random letters conveys a simple message. However, Daniel does not recognise yet the relationship between spoken language and the corresponding grapheme-phonemes. He does not understand the mapping of those words as whole units of meaning to the corresponding phonemes. At present Daniel is not making the connections between his aural, oral and visual concepts of how words as text are constructed. For example (in Figure 1.1) Daniel's sentence of 'My dog licks you' is represented as:

'p i p r r p a p r i r r r e p'.

Figure 1.1   Daniel's drawing of his dog and baseline writing

It is significant that Daniel in his baseline sentence does not use any letters from his name in any recognisable order. This indicates that Daniel has not yet internalised the construction of his name as a group of letters.

Approaches to spelling/writing development

In addressing the development of early years writing the practitioner should be aware of the learning needs of the child as the child develops as an emerging writer in a highly complex problem-solving activity (Flower et al. 1986; Scardamalia & Bereiter 1986). The complexity of the structural and developmental processes needed to become a writer requires that the child is taught not within a predominantly whole-class structure with its demands for completion within fast-paced time limits. The emerging writer requires sustained recursive opportunities to engage with the experiences which take the child from the steps of 'mark making' to the abstractions of written composition. This complexity is identified by Graham, Harris and Mason (2005) in that its development depends on changes in children's strategic behaviour, knowledge and motivation (p. 207). Allied to this it is now recognised that 'skilled writing for what it is, is a tremendously complex problem-solving act involving memory, planning, text generation and revision' (Bruning & Horn 2000, p. 26). The whole child cannot change alone 'if classroom instruction offers superficial [whole-class] low level tasks it is doubtful if children will engage in thoughtful and strategic ways' (Paris & Paris 2001, p. 93). However, 'many teachers struggle to understand how children develop writing skill, when writing instruction should begin and how to organise and implement an individualised writing programme' (Bloodgood 2002, in Martin et al. 2005, p. 236). Equally central to this complexity is 'the central guiding nurturing force of the teacher whose conceptions of writing will provide a model for and shape [children's] beliefs. We argue that programmes for developing writing will rest on the beliefs that teachers themselves hold' (Bruning & Horn 2000, p. 26). For children to become strategic and have an understanding and awareness of their own learning requirements, optimal conditions require that the children are trained as self-regulated learners (Graham & Harris 2000; Perry et al. 2007; Schunk & Zimmerman 1997). The Vygotskyian style is at the heart of [these] interactions as learners actively construct knowledge (Vanderburg 2006, p. 375). 'This recognises the importance of the interactions of ... teacher-student discourse in the classroom' (Vygotsky 1962, in Arapaki & Zafrana 2004, p. 45). However, children do not independently arrive at this position and this demands that teachers change from a didactic to a more child-centred pedagogy that leads to the recognition of a child's zone of proximal development (Vygotsky 1962).

A creative approach was adopted to facilitate the highly complex process of writing development. The use of a play/literacy connection (socio-dramatic play) serves to unlock and support the child's writing/spelling development. The child is being supported in his development by the teacher strategically easing the cognitive load – in this case, through scribing for the child. As the child's working memory expands he is capable of taking on board more of the 'writing requirements' and is supported to achieve automaticity as a writer. The 'more knowledgeable writers become – in content, in genre, in linguistic skills – the less effort they need for the planning and implementation process' (Becker 2004, p. 25).

The decision was made to use the strategy of socio-dramatic play as the framework for the intervention with Daniel. Hall and Robinson (1998) recognise the low status of play 'to a large extent it is still viewed by society ... as a non-educational process ... school is for learning not playing' (p. 2). Similarly, Christie (1991) argues that this misconception of play and the learning of literacy is caused by teachers thinking they must 'limit the amount of play because they don't fully understand how to legitimately use play to accomplish educational objectives' (p. 200). Since the Foundation Stage Early Years framework (2008) the profile of play has been more integrated into a learning concept – however, Siraj-Blatchford and Manni (2008) state that 'structured planned play opportunities often fall between two extremes – too much adult involvement in planning without child involvement in the origination of the activity, or alternatively, left totally unstructured with no clear understanding of the learning potential of the play activity' (p. 17). However, Christie is equally definite that 'play offers a chance to be literate' (Christie 1991, p. 22).

The early work of Chomsky and Read in the 1970s recognised the conceptualisation of spelling as a writing developmental process. Heald-Taylor (1998) takes this further by recognising that 'learning to spell is a complex, intricate, cognitive and linguistic process' (p. 405). These fundamental understandings are important in shaping appropriate expectations and instruction. In order for this to take place, a growing knowledge of developmental stages, in this instance, semi-phonetic spelling needs to be examined.

O'Sullivan (2000) argues that 'stage models of learning to spell have not been helpful to teachers in teaching spelling' (p. 9). She suggests further through her case studies that 'rather than spelling development passing through discrete stages … children begin to draw on several different sources of knowledge' (p. 10).

Heald-Taylor (1998) asserts that developmental stages 'Appear somewhat sequential, they are not static nor fixed; indeed there is considerable overlap between the stages. Moreover, it is folly to suggest that all children will move sequentially from one stage to the next' (p. 408).

Read (1986) argues against a precise developmental sequence but favours an outline of spelling development (p. 118). Morris and Templeton (2000) offer an interesting balance as they interpret the stage models of spelling development as not creating negative labels that are inflexible and rigid; they offer a starting point for instruction. Read's (1986) study of 32 children in pre-school and kindergarten's early spelling attempts to 'provide a window on their spelling processes' (cited in Read 1986, p. 2).

Read (1986) explores children's invented spellings and states that 'in representing their speech in letters, they are truly applying phonics in an authentic context' (in Templeton & Morris 1999, p. 108). Similarly, Sipe (2001) recognises that children who engage in invented spelling discover relationships by themselves about sounds and letters (p. 265). Wilde (1992) reminds the reader that 'invented spellings are a sign of linguistic and intellectual development' (p. 63). However, caution is necessary as invented spelling as a concept may falsely imply that it is a stage in the developmental process. Bean and Bouffler (1987) indicate that it is a strategy that all writers employ (p. 85). Templeton and Morris (1999) support this by suggesting that invented spelling continues throughout our lives – whenever we take a risk or 'have a go' (p. 108). The problem according to Routman (1993) is in invented spelling being misinterpreted by teachers who see 'Sounding out as the only strategy ... and teachers [are] not allowed to interfere with children's writing' (cited in Miller 2002, p. 33).

In classrooms studied by Clarke (1988) the teachers seem to have not commented on the correctness of the children's spellings. Treiman (1993) observed the same patterns in her classroom study and reported that: 'The teacher did not discuss how the children's spellings differed from the conventional ones and did not help the child to improve his/her spellings'. Sipe (2001) provides a fitting example of a child who spells conventionally for her reading support teacher yet does not do so in class – as she explains: 'My teacher gives me a break, she just wants me to come close' (p. 264). Wilde (1992) argues beyond 'a phonological strategy and a more direct visual/orthographic one' (p. 25) and strongly advocates the introduction of cognitive dissonance (p. 37). This is why modelling, that is, seeing letters, words, sentences and paragraphs in print, is so important for children. For example, modelling a daily sentence which has been originated orally by the children – essentially a detailed and complex structural activity – becomes a fun exploration of language in action. This can be developed further through the introduction of comprehension skills, for example higher-order thinking strategies. Such interrogatives as 'who', 'what', 'why' and 'where', and asking children to pose those questions to their peers to model their use and application in real contexts. This strategic intervention is supported by Montgomery (1997) who argues that a sole emphasis on phonics 'ignores the true speed of eye and brain, which enables us simultaneously to spell by ear and read by eye' (p. 9).

Socio-dramatic play to support early writing

Christie's previous statement of how to use play legitimately to accomplish learning objectives leads the debate on to symbolic play. Isenberg and Jacob (1983) provide a clear understanding of how; 'Symbolic play as a process of transforming an object ... situation or event through the use of motor and verbal actions ... provides an important source for literacy development' (in Hall & Robinson 1998, p. 8).

Wilford (2000) states that developing symbolic processes, for example a fantasy character, 'underpins the realisation that a written word stands for a spoken word and letters alone or in combination can represent sounds' (p. 1). Pellegrini and Galda (1991) state that 'symbolic representations are the best predictors of emergent writing'. These statements provide a conducive basis for developing a child's spelling, which also recognises and acknowledges that learning should be fun, stress free and enjoyable, particularly for very young children. Hughes (1999) in reminding us that 'the brain is proficient at remembering anything that is emotional, unusual, exaggerated or dramatic' (p. 40) provides a platform for understanding the relevance of transcription for 'novice' writers, that is, a five-year-old engaging with written symbols.

Myhill (2006) criticises the current teacher-centred pedagogy which still focuses largely on a legacy model based on the linear National Literacy Strategy Framework in which the objectives rather than the child's real or re-enacted experiences control the language programme. The dominant pedagogical model throughout the period has been and still is that of substantial whole-class teaching which Myhill (2006) suggests causes an 'orientation towards coverage and elicitation of facts rather than the creation and co-construction of interconnected learning' (p. 34) and evidences no 'substantial use of progressive child-centred methods' (Gammage 1987, p. 105), The Organisation for Economic Co-operation Development (OECD) survey of 15 classrooms found that 'in general the pedagogy was not focused on the observed interests of the children but sought to interest them in the concerns of the teacher' (2004, p. 59). In summary, what the OECD team observed was a teacher-centred rather than a child-centred pedagogy characterised by 'a focus on literacy and numeracy related activities, with evaluation criteria narrowly focused on cognitive outcomes and the early introduction of written symbolisation' (OECD 2004, p. 59). Teachers are not converting those objectives from the Framework into children's interests. Cook (2000) signals the need to build a bridge between play and the learning of cognitive skills (p. 74). For example, Price (1988) working with a group of nursery-age children constructed a large model of a ladybird after reading the 'Bad Tempered Ladybird'. He observed that the children: 'Appeared to collude that it was real and constantly talked about it as if it was real ... an ideal opportunity to incite some letter writing' (in Hall 1991, p. 2). In response to a party invitation from the ladybird, four-year-old Joel wrote (p. 11):

'UKNCCMtomypt'

(you can come to my party)

Here Joel is demonstrating elements of a semi-phonetic speller (Gentry 1982), and the context provided for the learning activity is both meaningful and fun. 'The children had gained significant insights into the conventions of written dialogue' (Price 1988, p. 13, in Hall (1991)). This example demonstrates the benefits to language learning and writing development of the integration of the affective and cognitive domains in the teacher's strategic planning. The example reinforces Christie's (1991) opening statement that 'play offers a chance to be literate' (p. 22). Similarly, Reifel and Neves (2000) looked at the writing behaviour of five-year-old children during their role play interactions and found that 'the children generated 337 graphemes during their interactions over a three-week period' (in Pellegrini 2000, p. 3) – a number which is well in excess of normal expectation. Cook's (2000) eight-week project involving 12 reception children highlights the importance of insightful teacher intervention. For example, the teacher introduced a complication into the role-play situation and observed that 'children demonstrated greatly increased confidence in emergent and orthographic approaches to writing … especially children who refused to write' (p. 76). A study by Korat, Bahar and Snapir (2002) focused on this important aspect of teacher intervention in the pursuit of literacy/play. Their six-month study involved 32 children aged five in Tel Aviv. Their investigation was carried out in a kindergarten class with a team of three teachers following Vygotsky's theory of play (attribution of higher mental functions to social dialogue). They wanted to build a developmentally appropriate play-based literacy model for pre-schoolers that could be used by future teachers. The purpose of the study was to determine the appropriate intervention for literacy to emerge. The teachers set up three levels of intervention. They included two areas of socio-dramatic play. These two areas were an easily accessible print-rich environment and an area where the children could get responses to questions initiated through their play. The last intervention was planning a curriculum that dealt with literacy. The children recognised and incorporated the written language into their imaginary worlds (Korat et al. 2002). Korat et al. found that the teacher's careful questions, prompts and suggestions 'encourage children to take risks and try their self-invented spelling by fostering children's socio-dramatic play' (p. 387). Korat et al. state that 'the emergence of literacy demands intervention' (p. 387) and requires that teachers should facilitate the play situation. Santrock (2006) observed teachers, through Vygotsky's zone of proximal development (ZPD), helping children to raise their cognitive and emotional development to a higher level by intervening in the play process. ZPD involves a more skilled individual assisting a child to achieve a task too difficult for them to master alone. The results of the observation data revealed a significant increase in cognitive behaviours during the child-directed play in groups when compared with teacher-directed frontal management.

There have been concerns expressed in the literature. Hall and Robinson (1998) suggest that creating role-play situations with specific learning outcomes may be perceived as 'manipulative and interventionist' (p. 47). Sutton-Smith (1995) argues that there may be negative aspects of play and literacy, for example, 'a child may ridicule a peer's use of emergent writing during play' (cited in Roskos & Christie 2001, p. 83). Compare this with Treiman's (1993) stress on the importance of guided invented spelling fostering the individual child's sensitivity and Wilde's (1992) celebration of invented spelling as a sign of linguistic and intellectual development (p. 63). Teachers have to be explicit in this process which allows children to be fully aware of what they are positively achieving by providing contextual situations that include the earlier statements of Hughes (1999), in which optimal learning is best achieved through anything 'that is emotional, unusual, exaggerated or dramatic' (p. 40).

Methodology

The focus of the case study was one child in a Liverpool school and an exploration of the strategies used by the child as a pre-alphabetic speller. The researcher/author who worked with Daniel used the vehicle of a socio-dramatic context within the child's play scenarios, and within that context introduced five specific teaching strategies: hearing, identifying, segmenting, blending and representing letter sounds in a written format (Depree & Iversen 1994).

A fantasy character and context was introduced (a ball with a face drawn on, a bed, furniture, food, etc). In session 1 the author engaged with the child's own 'lived experience' as a means of starting off the active intervention. The aim was to encourage Daniel to talk about his pet animal (dog). This was introduced by the author talking to Daniel about her cat and then Daniel described the dog which he had at home. He did this with great animation and enthusiasm. This first session was focused on generating a scenario centred around his pet. Daniel's independent descriptive sentence about his dog is shown in Figure 1.1.

In session 2 the author produced a box and told Daniel 'someone lives in that box'. Daniel was excited and wanted to find out who it was. He opened the box and found, to his delight, a ball. Daniel took the ball out of its box and laid the table for the ball with pretend food, napkins, cutlery, etc. The scenario was extended through prompts such as 'it's dinnertime for the ball. What does the ball have to eat?' This led to conversational interplay between Daniel, the ball and the author. Daniel and the author set out lunch for the ball. After the ball had its lunch, Daniel decided to write a sentence about the ball's activity. The author provided a blank sheet of paper for Daniel to work with. He drew the ball (visual connection) and then retold the story to the author. The author then scribed the sentence, emphasising to Daniel the dominant phonemes within each word (hearing connection). Daniel then pointed with his finger (directionality) at one-to-one correspondence with the words in the author's sentence. He then was asked to write his sentence. 'Let's start with the first word. What sound can you hear in "my"?' This process was repeated throughout the whole sentence. This structured approach of aural training in careful phonemic isolation and segmentation resulted in Daniel's conceptual leap to demonstrating his own consonant framework using initial and medial phonemes, for example Macdonalds represented as 'm' and 'd'. The progression from Daniel's sentence in Figure 1.1 to his output in Figure 1.2 evidences this, and it is noteworthy that at no stage was Daniel asked to copy a modelled sentence.

In session 3 the author introduced a second character, a three-inch teddy bear; this further fascinated Daniel and opened opportunities for further rich dialogue. Consequently, Daniel created a scenario in which the teddy and the

Figure 1.2   My ball likes to play Macdonald's

ball were involved in having a fight (see Figure 1.3). The story originated in an oral re-enactment by Daniel of the 'fight'. Daniel demonstrates increased confidence through lexical choice and exposition: 'Teddy scratched the ball' and the use of character dialogue, 'Send teddy to bed'. Daniel uses the same methodological approach as in session 2. As Daniel is demonstrating that he cannot spell the word 'the', the author introduced a kinaesthetic approach to incorporating the word 'the' within his working memory. Daniel was not pressured into writing the newly acquired word (as his sentence was already written) but it was his next step as a writer. The word 'the' was written out, cut up and re-arranged by Daniel into the correct sequence, signalling the importance of spelling strategies that go beyond an emphasis on sound alone (Moustafa & Dombey 1998).

In session 4 Daniel follows the sequence of his story begun in session 3. The ball has been hurt in the fight with teddy so must go to the doctor.

Figure 1.3   Teddy scratched the ball. 'Send teddy to bed!'

Figure 1.4 evidences that Daniel has assimilated his high frequency word 'the' and moved it to the forefront of his writing. The newly acquired definite article dominates his sentence visually at the expense of his placement of the other words in the sentence. Once Daniel starts to internalise the high frequency word and no longer places the burden on working memory his style will revert to a regular pattern of sentence structure.

In session 5 Daniel continues the scenario (fight between teddy and the ball) with the doctor putting a plaster on the ball (Figure 1.5).

Daniel is now so confident as a writer (balance of affective and cognitive support by the author) that he is demonstrating his new sight word (the) and his initiative in the creative content and secure structure of his sentence. This can be seen in this transcript of the conversation between Daniel and the teacher:

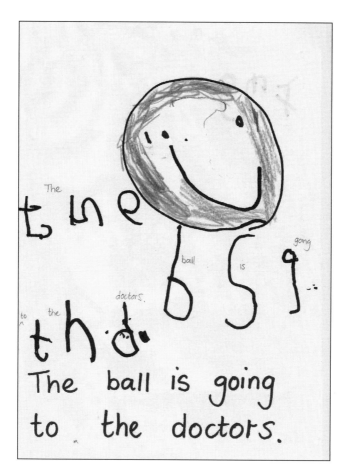

Figure 1.4   The ball is going to the doctors

Daniel: The ball has got blood on the top.

Teacher: What do you think we should do?

Daniel: Sometimes I be sick and I go to the doctor's.

Teacher: What happens there?

Daniel: Can I write I am sick to the doctor?

It is interesting that during this exchange the teacher prompts appeared to have no effect on his line of thought. Daniel has his own agenda and these interest areas are uppermost in his mind.

Figure 1.5   The doctor put a plaster on the ball

Conclusion

This research project was based on the theory that 'good teaching forces diff-erentiation' (Perrenoud 1998) and the researcher/author planned a series of interventions that matched the learning needs of the writer. Perrenoud, one of the original formative teaching and learning theorists, recognises the cen-trality of the individual in teaching and learning. 'To the extent that children do not have the same abilities, nor the same needs or the same way of working, an optimal situation for one pupil will not be optimal for another' (Perrenoud 1998, pp. 93–94).

At the beginning of the research Daniel showed the tendencies of a pre-alphabetic writer with little understanding of the relationship between spo-ken language and the corresponding grapheme phonemes. As he progressed through the short (five teaching sessions) programme of exposure to socio-dramatic play opportunities, his writing developed and he demonstrated an ability to represent spoken language mapped to the corresponding pho-nemes. So how was this progress made? The author had determined a strat-egy focused on the integration of socio-dramatic play alongside language, illustrations (to support the exploration of meaning) and sounds. This strat-egy provided meaningful situations to unlock Daniel's learning potential and recognises the importance of play in early years settings. This learning strat-egy is fundamentally 'complex, intricate and cognitively demanding' (Heald-Taylor 1998, p. 405) and based on fun and enjoyment. This research shows the significance of creating educational objectives in a manner that demon-strates 'proficiency to learning anything that is emotional, unusual, exagger-ated or dramatic' (Hughes 1999, p. 40).

For the transmission of these messages from this small-scale research (i.e. an understanding of the child and his/her learning needs, the sequential steps in that learning and the ability to plan multi-modal experiences to sup-port that learning) to the wider audience of the (early years) teaching profes-sion, there needs to be an appreciation by the teacher that learning involves the whole child's development. This requires balanced support for the affec-tive and cognitive domains of the child. This demands that teachers have a theoretical construct of learning with the child at the centre rather than the current teacher-centred pedagogy which focuses on linear planning and a one-size-fits-all methodology (Boyle & Charles 2009).

> Pedagogy is the observable act of teaching together with its attendant discourse of educational theories, values, evidence and justifications. It is what one needs to know and the skills one needs to command in order to make and justify the many different kinds of decisions of which teaching is constituted. (Alexander 2008, p. 29)

CHAPTER 2

HOW COLLABORATION DEVELOPS EARLY YEARS WRITING SKILLS

Introduction

This chapter investigates the development of major aspects of writing development such as collaboration, the importance of peer interactions, social learning and the fusion of illustrations, talk and writing to assist children's communication and understanding. The collaboration of the two girls ('Liz' and 'Jane') as writers was tracked through four teaching interventions in which the girls chose the genre (narrative – folk tale) and developed the visual and writing aspects with equal status through this multi-modal approach. We relate Liz's development in story writing and the progress that she made in achieving text cohesion, spelling development and ideation through a collaborative writing process. The case study investigates the integration of major aspects of writing development such as collaboration (co-construction), the importance of peer interactions through social learning and the fusion of illustrations and writing to assist children's communication and understanding – all essential elements of formative teaching and learning. We examine the rationale for the inclusion of collaborative peer-assisted writing and peer interaction as a social writing process, supporting the young writer's affective domain development. The strengths and complexities of peer interaction, the role of illustrations and their positive impact on composition are discussed.

What is collaborative writing?

Collaborative writing is one of the processes in the social construction of learning. Vygotsky stated that 'learning is socially constructed during interaction with others and the relationship between literacy and social interaction is complex and significant to their learning' (Vygotsky 1978, p. 243).

To exemplify this: A teacher has just finished reading a story to a class of six-year-olds. After talking about what was interesting and exciting she then says: 'Now I want you to imagine that you are that character and write a story about it in your best handwriting, quietly in your seats'. This scene is familiar to some infant classrooms and appears relatively straightforward and unproblematic.

This teaching scenario vignette assumes that children will produce good stories written alone, quietly and with no discussion. 'They are cajoled into "writing better" without knowing how good writing unfolds or how a writer thinks' (Graves 1994, p. 46). It may be true that the writing process comes easily and uncomplicated to some children, however, Fisher and Williams (2000, p. 70) remind us that story writing for children: 'provides them with the most complex of intellectual challenges'. Hodges (2002, p. 9) recognises the 'problem of writing individually as it creates tension of what to write and composing the whole story'. Our premise is that 'peer collaboration provides a means of sharing the cognitive load involved in text composition' (Graves 1983, p. 84) and transcription. The cognitive load is a critical aspect in children's language development and one in which the 'load' is lessened when collaboration is utilised as a legitimate strategy.

Understanding collaborative (peer-assisted) writing

Topping (2001) suggests that collaborative writing helps participants to structure their thoughts. He suggests that collaborative or paired writing supports the following higher order skills: 'planning, intelligent questioning, reorganisation and restructuring to counterbalance the traditional focus on mechanics and the final product' (p. 142). The paired writing model as proposed by Topping (2001) has much to offer in terms of embracing the social aspects of writing and the value of co-composition. However, the model presented in its entirety appears quite complicated for practitioners, with six steps, ten questions, five stages and four levels (Topping 2001, p. 4). This model supports the thinking of Graves (1983, 1994); Bereiter and Scardamalia (1987) and Whitehead (1997) in that 'the interaction of two … reduces head scratching, dithering and blind panic at the sight of a blank piece of paper … with a great emphasis on continuity, the pair stimulating each other to keep on going at any threatened hiatus …' (Topping 2001, p. 142). Furthermore, the action research carried out by Topping, Yarrow, Sutherland and Nixon (2000, in Topping 2001) highlights the effectiveness of paired writing. The Nixon project (1991) involved five-year-old emergent writers and found that 'they were writing more independently, and offering more and better ideas for writing' (cited in Topping 2001, p. 166). The Yarrow project (2000) involved 28

10-year-olds with behaviour difficulties as part of two control groups, that is, one group that wrote alone and another that wrote in pairs. The results indicated that 'paired writers showed significant greater gains than children who wrote alone … paired writers also showed more positive self-esteem as writers than those that wrote alone' (Topping 2001, p. 166). 'In school, learning to write is reduced to conquering a code, the exercise becomes a surface imitation of genres and text-types …' (Nilsson 2010, p. 2). Instead of being founded on and around the needs and interests of children as they naturally develop and on their activity, 'writing is given to them from without, from the teacher's hands. This situation recalls the development of a technical skill such as piano playing: the pupil develops finger dexterity and learns to strike the keys while reading music, but he is no way involved in the essence of the music itself (Vygotsky 1978). Literacy in educational contexts 'is most often approached as a motor skill and not as a complex social, cultural and creative activity' (Nilsson 2010, p. 2).

Through integrating the above collaborative activities in their pedagogy, teachers should move away from an over-reliance on the mechanics of written composition.

Underpinning the successful development of the emerging writer is the crucial importance of talk and communication through collaboration. Zhoa (2003) reminds us that a 'traditional stance of writing as a solitary (if not silent) activity needs to be dismissed and the opportunities for talk should be understood as an extremely important part of the composing process' (p. 1). Essential as talk may be, a certain amount of prudence must also be applied; Wong (2002) recognises its importance but states that 'the opportunity is offered but taken up unequally as some will stay tight lipped' (p. 1). The complexity and the multi-modality of the collaborative writing process is identified by Graves, who analysed teachers and children at work as writers. In his work he described writing as 'a complex process rather than a single event, with great emphasis placed upon "rehearsal" for writing: day dreaming, sketching, doodling, making lists, outlining, reading, conversing, thinking about the product' (Graves 1983, p. 221). Graves is referring in his use of the term complexity to 'the complex distinctions writers must make between written and oral texts'. (Graves 1983, p. 9). To reinforce this important pedagogical strategy, O'Sullivan (2000) recognises how young children need to understand how to move from oral language to the written word and identifies the teacher as a key figure in this process (p. 11).

The teacher's role in collaborative writing

The teacher has to understand the importance of collaborative writing to children's writing development. It will not happen otherwise. The teacher has to provide the links and the development of oral and written language and, in particular, a conducive environment which promotes social learning through collaborative writing.

For Topping (2001) training 'children to work in collaboration becomes a necessity, for he maintains that many schools believe they promote collaborative learning when all they actually do is to place students together and hope for the best' (p. 166). Topping's quote alerts us to the importance of the teacher understanding her/his role and children similarly understanding their roles in what is a complex process. Perrenoud (1998) talks about the deregulation of the roles in the learning relationship and we demonstrate below how this can be exemplified in the collaborative writing process.

Teachers need to understand more about the dynamics of writing groups (ability, age, friendship, gender, ethnicity, SES factors) (Smit, 1989) and be mindful of the socio-moral context in which peer learning occurs. If less able children are paired with more/less able peers', this is a climate of deficiency/ superiority created on the part of the less/more able children (Delisi 2002). Teachers need to understand that in designing collaborative activities they are making statements about 'who' the children are socially and academically and need to be aware of the power they have in creating negative messages for children about their worth as literate individuals (Kesner & Matthews 2003). They need to be aware that these factors are so powerful that they may override the pedagogical intent of the writing activities (Smagorinsky & O'Donnell-Allen 2000).

The children in Wiseman's study (2003) not only wrote collaboratively but were taught in a collaborative classroom. The teacher 'created an environment that allowed for social exchanges and collaboration'. The outcome of this was an observation of two girls who were able to 'scaffold and develop their abilities through a joint activity' (Wood et al. 2001, p. 104). 'They regularly chose to talk together, to plan what they were going to write together [co-construction]. Their stories would evolve from their talking, drawing and writing' (Wiseman 2003, p. 804) and demonstrate the interconnectedness of drawing, talking and writing. These three elements are very important and cannot be dismissed as mere irrelevancies, although they are often derogatorily linked to children being perceived as wasting time. Wiseman exemplifies the necessity for teachers to understand the deregulation and observes that 'students' composing processes [are] creative, messy, collaborative and talkative; the room buzzes with voices and movement' (p. 804).

Multiple roles of children in collaborative writing

The collaborative roles that the children adopt as paired writers tend to be that one is labelled a 'helper' and the other as a 'writer' (Topping 2001). There is fluidity in the roles as both children in the collaborative process move in and out of those roles at different stages of the co-composition. Both children are simply writers in pursuit of writing a story.

There are four possible models of learning situations for the collaborative writing relationship:

1. child working alone, then joined by another child (peer) as collaborator (co-construction);
2. child working alone, then joined by teacher as collaborator (co-construction);
3. child working with child (peer) collaborator with minimal teacher intervention (co-construction); and finally
4. child working with child (peer) but with major teacher intervention (co-construction).

In our study Figures 2.1 and 2.2 demonstrate model 2, that is the child joined by the teacher, Figures 2.3 and 2.4 shift the model to child and peer collaboration with minimal teacher intervention.

The teacher's role is pivotal in understanding the possibilities of these different types of working relationships and creating a particular kind of atmosphere and tone that encourages and maintains positive interactions and children's exchanges.

Visual literacy as integral to the composing process

'The artwork facilitates the writing process, resulting in a text that is richer in sensory detail and more intricate than the most traditional writing-first crayon drawing-second approach' (Andrzejczak et al. 2005, p. 2).

Marsh and Millard (2001, p. 55) trace a low esteem for visual literacy by suggesting that: 'teachers largely regard the movement from pictures to words as one of intellectual progression'. This assumes that drawing is reduced to a stage that children will eventually discard as their writing becomes more sophisticated. However, we feel that the opposite should apply. Ernst (1994) 'states that the relationship between seeing, telling, drawing and writing is intimate, essential and a significant aspect of teaching the writing act' (p. 176).

Marsh and Millard (2001) found that 'children appeared to use drawings in an integral way in their written work and there was a strong dialogic relationship between word and image'.

Differences were found between groups of children who drew before their writing and those that did not in a study by Norris, Kouider and Reichard (2002). They found that 'drawing became an effective planning strategy … as a reference point to prompt them towards what should come next in their writing.

The importance of visual literacy is emphasised by researchers such as Andrzejczak, Trainin and Poldberg (2005). Andrzejczak et al.'s study (2005) utilises examples of children's outstanding visual and written outcomes produced as a result of the intrinsic enjoyment of the art-making process which attracted the children into writing. Therefore the art making became the hook into the academic endeavours of writing.

Case study methodology: Jane and Liz, collaborative writers

This case study is an analysis of one child, 'Jane' aged six, and her development process in collaborative writing. It focuses on peer collaboration as a 'means of providing insight and inspiration' (Beaman 1999). Furthermore, Topping's 'paired writing model has much to offer in embracing the social aspects of writing and the value of co-composition' (Topping 2001, p. 162). We explore the four possible models given on p. 26.

The use of a peer offers an alternative pathway for writing development because the child is offered access to correct word structures, coherence and story ideas.

Jane was selected because from our observations she was demonstrating disengagement during writing sessions. However, in small-group discussion, Jane contributed imaginatively to oral narratives. Her written work did not demonstrate the latent potential of her oral work (Jane appeared to be locked into single phonemic representations as word construction) and we hoped to scaffold Jane onto the next 'stage' in the writing process. At the start of the study we set up an activity to explore Jane's starting point as a writer (see Figure 2.1). To initiate this we had a discussion with Jane about her favourite stories.

Jane: I like writing stories with animals in, they're cuddly and funny.

Authors: Can you think of something funny to write about?

Jane: Well erm, not really.

Authors: What about if I write your ideas down, then you will know where to start.

Jane: OK, once upon a time there lived a girl called 'Mr Bear'. She liked being called 'Mr' because it made her different. She had a friend called 'Piggy' who laughed so much he kept falling over. One day they went to the sweet shop to buy red and green jellies. Piggy saw himself in the mirror and laughed so much that he dropped the jellies on the floor. 'Let's go home', said Mr Bear, then they went to bed.

Authors: I really like your characters …that's a really interesting way to describe the girl in your story … let's see if you can write a story with those wonderful characters, I'd love to see what they look like.

The story that Jane wrote as a result of this baseline discussion (see Figure 2.1) includes Mr Bear and Piggy but does not reflect or indeed include all the details and character development that she had orally narrated. Jane at this stage was incapable of including all these details in her writing as they were too demanding on her cognitive load and working memory (Becker 2004). The illustration is also informative as Jane merely draws Mr Bear and Piggy but ignores the detail, for example sweet shop, sweets, mirror and the bed.

Figure 2.1   Jane's first baseline story

Transcription

Once upon a time there lived a girl called Mr Bear. She liked being called mister because it made her different. She had a friend called piggy who laughed so much he kept falling over. One day they went to the sweet shop to buy red and green jellies. Piggy saw himself in the mirror and laughed so much that he dropped the jellies on the floor. Let's go home said Mr Bear. Then they went to bed.

Jane's writing in Figure 2.1 shows that she is attempting to write within, but is not secure at, the initial phonemic stage because of her sound-letter inconsistencies. She does not spell correctly any of the high frequency words in this first piece. Her writing evidences that she is struggling for consistency with phoneme-grapheme mapping, still moving in and out of that stage. For example, she spells 'bear' on her first attempt as 'bui' and on her second attempt as 'boc' and her third attempt is 'bio'. She is guessing at the unstressed vowels and knows that there are several letters to correctly represent those sounds but she does not know what they look like. Her meta-linguistic understanding is insufficient to make those decisions as 'sounding out' as a single strategy is not sufficient to help her. 'Spelling is never purely visual – orthographic representations of words are created by mapping them onto their spoken word counterparts' (Berninger et al., 2006, p. 65). Jane is now ready to be supported with a strategy that goes beyond reliance on sounds (phonics). 'Once mapping relationships between phonology and orthography for words are learned, an autonomous orthographic lexicon begins to be constructed, in which orthographic word forms are represented independent of phonological word forms' (Berninger et al., 2006, p. 65). This is about Jane being supported, for example through exposure to the more capable peer (Vygotsky 1978), modelling also with the

Figure 2.2   Jane's second baseline story

teacher contextualising activities and using visual strategies (multimodalities, multiliteracies[1]: Vorvilas et al. 2010).

To confirm Jane's starting point, we initiated a second piece of writing. This was again focused on a story originated by Jane from her own areas of interests (see Figure 2.2).

Transcription

Once upon a time there was a girl [child's story became undecipherable]

Having observed the writing behaviours of Jane in both sessions, we noted that this second piece shows a clear visual decline in presentation, that is, the writing is vertical, list-like, unlike the mature left–right directionality demonstrated in the first piece. There is a regression evident in Jane's cohesion, spelling and lack of detail in the illustration. Clearly this reinforces the difficulties of transcription (spelling) and translation (text production) which for Jane appear to be obscuring her capability for developing a coherent story (Berninger 2001; Steffler et al. 1998). There are too many skill demands and these have contributed to a decline in motivation as Jane cannot see 'success' in what she is writing. In Figure 2.2, the illustration (in contrast to Figure 2.1) is located in disconnect from the story at the end of the page. The illustration lacks detail, conviction and authority (compare with the illustration in Figure 2.1) and contributes to our concerns about Jane's motivation and desire to write.

Following the baseline pieces (written during sessions 1 and 2) we introduced Liz as a collaborator for Jane. We had identified Jane's friend, Liz, as demonstrating mature language development which would be a positive factor for Jane's progress. In the next two sessions the children worked together and co-composed. We determined that 'by providing the children with opportunities to express themselves in many modalities – through words and metaphors, colours, drawing, sound, music and movement' (Nielsen 2009, p. 83) their role was *not* restricted. The sequence of the sessions was: first, setting up the oral rehearsal (children's storytelling), secondly scribing the story map text as the children drew the picture sequences

---

[1]Multimodality refers to the simultaneous reading, processing and/or producing and interacting with various modes of print, image, movement, graphics, animation, sound, music and gesture. In *Multiliteracies* the New London Group (2000, p. 9) argues that literacy pedagogy now must take account of the burgeoning variety of text forms associated with information and multimedia technologies.

and finally, the written co-composition by the children. The following conversation about which story they would write was initiated by Liz during teaching session 3:

Liz: Let's do the story we had by Miss about the 'three hags'.

Jane: Yeah, those witches were scary, I didn't like them.

Liz: Hags, NOT witches … I liked their black fingers.

Story Map

The three hags had black fingers that looked like sticks. They were nasty and evil, and guarded the fire so no-one could have it.

When the hags fell asleep a boy came along and robbed the fire. They caught him.

The boy threw the fire into the air and the frog caught the fire but his tail got burnt off. The frog threw the fire up into the air and Robin Red breast caught it on his chest.

Then the tree caught it and swollowed the fire inside its trunk and that's why it is brown now.

Figures 2.3a and 2.3b   The three hags story

Transcription of written story – The three hags

Once upon a time there lived three hags. Their fingers were like black sticks. A boy robbed some fire while the hags were asleep. The hags woke up and chased the boy. The hags caught the boy. The boy robbed the fire and the frog caught the fire. The frog's tail got burned off. Robin red-breast

(Continued)

(Continued)

caught the fire and burned his breast. The tree caught the fire and it stayed inside its body.

Picture 1. The three hags had black fingers that looked like sticks. They were nasty and evil and guarded the fire so no one could have it.

Picture 2. When the hags fell asleep a boy came along and robbed the fire. They caught him.

Picture 3. The boy threw the fire into the air and the frog caught the fire but his tail got burnt off. The frog threw the fire up into the air and Robin redbreast caught it on his chest.

Picture 4. Then the tree caught it and swallowed the fire inside its trunk and that is why it is brown now.

The children were supplied with a sheet of blank paper with four circles drawn as the planning templates for a story. The children were asked to draw two pictures each (coherence through the four planning circles) and to describe their section of the story for us to scribe (securing beginning, middle and end) (see Figure 2.3a). The illustrations became an integrated part of a multimodal strategy to support the children as they wrote the story (see Figure 2.3b – Jane's writing is in the lighter grey tint). In Jane's written version she demonstrates whole-word structures in sentences instead of just using initial phonemes. She starts to write with capital letters and full stops, showing an immediate improvement in punctuation. There is complete coherence in the story and its ideas. Some high frequency words are being spelt correctly, for example 'the'. There is inclusion of vowels in words and the vowels are used correctly, for example the 'o' in 'frog', the 'e' in 'red' and the 'o' in 'robin'. There are also close approximations when Jane does not manage exact accuracy, for example 'fire' spelt as 'fayr' is a plausible phonemic representation for a child this age (Depree & Iversen 1994). Jane's miscues are now much more plausible than in her baseline attempts. The process of scribing should be authentic, that is, the language of the child should be used rather than the teacher asking the child a few 'closed' questions and then writing in her own version. There is strong congruence between the author's story map scribing (from the children's oral narrative) in Figure 2.3a and the children's own written version of the story in Figure 2.3b. Similarly, unlike Jane's initial baseline solo effort (see Figure 2.1), the collaborative pair's detailed illustrated story map is congruent to their written story. On Figure 2.3b, the switching of authorship after each sentence provides coherence and a structure for development (Hochman 2002). Similarly, Figure 2.3b illustrates that with the appropriate scaffolding provided by peer collaboration, Jane's problems of transcription and translation are improved in the areas of text cohesion; Jane is long over-burdened with generating text ideas/events/actions etc. (Topping 2001). Throughout this collaborative working session, Jane consistently referred to what Liz had written to aid her spellings (co-construction). For example, her spelling of 'the' begins as 't' but is eventually by the end of the written piece refined to the correct spelling of the word. This is how young learners learn to spell from correctly contextualised modelling (Berninger et al. 2006). Within this collaborative process errors concerning correct sequences were quickly challenged:

Jane: My turn now, the frog caught the fire and the tree swallowed it …

Liz: Erm … No, it was robin red breast, then the tree … remember? … cos the frog got its tail burnt off first … then …

Jane: Oh yeah … I remember now.

This interjection prompted Jane to recall the events correctly and led Liz to point out that she had missed out the robin in her illustrations on their story map.

In teaching session 4, the final session of this piece of research, the class had been listening to stories on native Americans. The session followed the same format as the preceding one and illustrates the developing competence and confidence of Jane scaffolded by her peer. The shaping, developing and writing of a cohesive narrative is maintained and improved. When Jane's first piece of independent writing (Figure 2.1) is compared to her collaborative pieces (Figures 2.3a, 2.3b, 2.4a and 2.4b) there is evidence of her deeper understanding of structure (Topping 2001). The illustrations (visual literacy) similarly indicate this development in the children's language thinking and competence – the illustrations indicate how closely the children have become *involved* and *immersed* in their theme. The use of detail and the matching of colours (patternation) both indicate the motivation that the children feel and their understanding of the integration of the visual and the written. We had structured the process so that the children appreciated the sequence of first having a visual representation prior to writing, rather than the reverse, as happens in so many classroom situations.

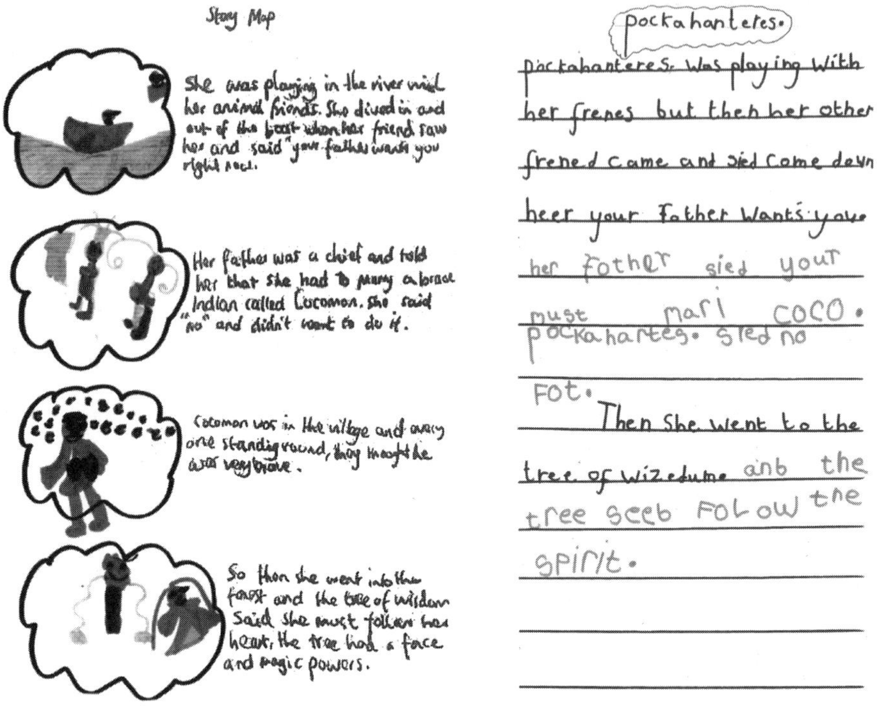

Story Map

She was playing in the river with her animal friends. She dived in and out of the boat when her friend saw her and said "your father wants you right now".

Her father was a chief and told her that she had to marry a brave Indian called Cocomon. She said "no" and didn't want to do it.

Cocomon was in the village and every one standing round, they thought he was very brave.

So then she went into the forest and the tree of wisdom said she must follow her heart, the tree had a face and magic powers.

pockahanteres.

Pockahanteres. Was playing with her frenes but then her other frened came and sied come down heer your Father Wants you. her Fother sied your must marI COCO. pockahartes. sied no Fot. Then She went to the tree of wizedume anb the tree seeb FoLow the spirit.

Figure 2.4a and 2.4b   Pocahontas story

Transcription of the written story: Pocahontas

Pocahontas was playing with friends but then her other friend came and said "Come down here, your father wants you". Her father said "You must marry Coco". Pocahontas said "no thanks". Then she went to the tree of wisdom. And the tree said "Follow the spirit".

Picture 1 She was playing in the river with animal friends. She dived in and out of the boat. When her friend saw her she said "Your father wants you right now".

Picture 2 Her father was a chief and told her that she had to marry a brave Indian called Cocomon. She said no and didn't want to do it.

Picture 3 Cocomon was in the village and everyone was standing around and they thought he was very brave.

Picture 4 So then she went into the forest and the tree of wisdom said she must follow her heart, the tree had a face and magic powers.

In this final piece the positive effects of peer modelling in relation to Jane's spelling development, text cohesion and story ideas demonstrate a more knowledgeable and confident writer. She has moved from representing words as initial phonemes to the conventions of sentence structure, that is, representing words as recognisable units (syntactically) arranged. Notably there are no word omissions. Equally interesting is that as Jane acquires higher order skills she regresses in her punctuation. This temporary loss of punctuation is part of the normal developmental process. Jane will spiral back into the correct punctuation skills as she continues to develop linguistically (Becker 2004).

Conclusion

The research evidences the role of collaborative writing in shaping an individual's writing development, especially in the areas of transcription and composition. Collaborative writing demonstrates growth in terms of the development of structure, the logical growth of ideas and the sharing of 'the cognitive burden of text composition through peer collaboration' (Graves 1994, p. 227).

The two co-composition sessions (Figures 2.3 and 2.4) demonstrate qualities of cognitive apprenticeship (Sadler 1998). The introduction of a peer (Liz) enabled the redefining of Jane's role as a writer, in short she wrote with more enthusiasm (affective domain) and purpose. Similarly, the two girls in Wiseman's (2003) study emphasise the multi-modal processes of writing by their integration of talking, drawing and writing. The effect of the multi-modal process is seen through the detailed story maps that Liz and Jane drew as they planned and structured their written narratives. This strategy was absent when Jane wrote independently and 'teachers need to understand, be conversant with and recognise the necessity of planning for the different semiotics spheres involved in creating the emerging writer' (Heydon 2007, p. 38).

Writing collaboratively, as evidenced through the co-compositions in Figures 2.3 and 2.4, the pair enjoyed talking and constructing text and challenges teachers whose construct of writing is that it is a solitary and silent activity (Nilsson 2010). Peer collaboration should be a key pedagogical strategy (Topping 2001). Clark (1976) reminds us that 'the way in which we teach is not necessarily the way in which children learn'.(cited in Whitehead 1997, p. 146)

Jane, on the evidence of the four-week strategy, benefited greatly from her collaborations with her peer. However, it is worth repeating that teachers need to be mindful of the socio-moral dynamics (Delisi 2002) that occur in peer collaborations – in this case, Liz was socially more adept than Jane, who herself was quite a popular member of the class, and these factors consequently raised Jane's own profile and credibility.

The challenges of collaborative writing are complex, before contemplating using the strategy the teacher needs to determine at what stage the child is located on the writing continuum. Which skills need to be taught, revisited or consolidated? How capable is the child of dealing with the interwoven linguistic and motivational demands of the complex relationship of writing with a collaborator? The strategy has clear potential in terms of individual growth to both teachers and children; to practitioners in their pedagogical strengthening and for children in the development of story writing. This states the positive outcomes of the research while not underestimating the limitations. The study involved a relatively small number of sessions, four in total, with each weekly session lasting approximately 35–40 minutes, so cannot nor does not claim to be conclusive nor representative. However, it does demonstrate that on 'a small scale it can be developed in [classrooms] with tangible results' (Salvetti 2001, p. 79). Another limitation concerns the child's perspective, for example comparing Jane's views of writing individually and then collaboratively would have produced attitudinal responses and also given evidenced validity and credence to collaborative writing.

In conclusion, the intention of this study is not to suggest that collaborative writing is the panacea for all writing progress or behaviours. However, it does have a significant place within the 'toolkit' of formative teaching, learning and assessment strategies and is one route to unlocking the potential of all children.

CHAPTER 3

THE IMPORTANCE OF MULTIMODALITY AND MULTILITERACIES IN DEVELOPING YOUNG COMMUNICATORS

Introduction

There's talking, photos, computer graphics, drawing, print, sign language, music, films. (Marlon, age 7, QCA 2004, p. 5)

The focus of this chapter is on the reception and production of language and the judicious use of multimodal strategies (audio recorder, visual skills of fairytale scenes, props) and peer collaboration in supporting one child's storytelling abilities using the genre of fairytales. For this purpose we use the genre of fairytales, a traditional mode of storytelling with young children. The basis of the discussion is that for children 'communication occurs through different but synchronous modes: language, print, images, graphics, movement, gesture, texture, music, sound' (Kress 2003, p. 51). These synchronous modes form an empirical definition of multimodality, 'a multimodal approach that looks beyond language to all forms of communication' (Jewitt et al. 2009, p. 11) and which highlight the potential complex interactions between media, modes and semiotic resources. To evidence the possibilities of using a multimodal teaching strategy for developing the communication skills through the storytelling of a five-year-old, we conducted the following research study in an inner city primary school in Liverpool.

Children love fairytales, and, according to the research of Marsh and Millard:

> Five key reasons for children's love of fairytales: one, they generally begin with 'once upon a time' and situate the story away from the context of the child. Secondly, they often end with 'and they lived happily ever after' so offering satisfactory closure. Thirdly, they have a basic bipolar structure which children find attractive – good/evil, handsome/ugly, kind/cruel – no ambiguity or ambivalence. Fourthly, they centre on the actions of heroes and heroines who are typical, not specific and so children can relate to them, and finally good and evil are omnipresent and the differences between them apparent. (Berger 1997, in Marsh and Millard 2000, p. 159)

Fairytales, as a genre of literature, have traditionally a long and somewhat turbulent history, particularly in their creation and interpretation. Indeed, as early as 1903 a book written by Dr Karl Oppel entitled the *Parent's Book: Practical Guidance for The Education at Home*, argued that 'fairy tales fill the imagination … with horror … terror and a belief in the supernatural' (cited in 'The History of Education and Childhood 1998, p. 2). Tatar (1999) recognised that 'cruelty and violence have been the signature of German fairy tales' (p. 212). One cannot argue that these elements do not exist in these narratives, indeed they do quite consistently, and this is precisely part of their appeal for children. Fairytales are indeed inextricably linked to the idea that all human beings tell stories. Hardy (1977) describes 'narrative as a primary act of mind' (cited in Gamble and Yates 2002, p. 20). She suggests that this act of storytelling is natural and this is how we make sense of our experiences. Koki (1998) takes this further by calling children the 'narrated selves of their own lives' (p. 1), in which stories are 'powerful fundamental forms for the mental organisation of experience arising in development with the onset of language, memory and mental imaging' (Fox 1993, p. 193). Clearly then, this implied innate ability to tell stories appears on the surface to be simple and unproblematic. Research suggests that 'the most valuable aspect of storytelling is that it gives children experience with de-contextualised language, requiring them to make sense of ideas that are about something beyond the here and now' (Beck & McKeown 2001, p. 10).

The basis of the discussion is that for children, 'communication occurs through different but synchronous modes: language, print, images, graphics, movement, gesture, texture, music, sound' (Kress 2003, p. 51). These synchronous modes form an empirical definition of multimodality, 'a multimodal approach that looks beyond language to all forms of communication' (Jewitt et al. 2009, p. 11) and which highlights the potential complex interactions between media, modes and semiotic resources with its inherent danger of sensory overload. To evidence the possibilities of using a multimodal teaching strategy for developing the communication skills through the storytelling of a five-year-old, we conducted the following research study in a medium sized (350 pupils) inner city primary school in Liverpool. This allows for detailed investigation of the interaction between changes in technology, policy, curriculum and pupil learning resources. As teachers we need to understand, be comfortable with, and use efficiently in support of learning 'the many and complex modes and various settings in which communication is effected and meaning is synthesised' (Katsarou & Tsafos 2010, p. 53).

Over the past 15 years or so, the interactions of teachers and pupils have changed in significant ways and remained the same in equally significant ways. The teacher now uses the interactive white board as a main resource, and has instantaneous access to and use of image, colour and layout to an extent which was not available 10 years ago. In the main, however, children's classroom experiences within current pedagogical styles are still based on mono-modality (Goouch 2008; Myhill 2006; Wyse et al., 2007) and on a didactic pedagogy (Alexander & Flutter 2009; Boyle & Charles 2010a). For example, theories of reading and writing instruction are based on the child reading mono-modal or print-based text. Case study research by Nilsson (2010) explored the written outcomes of 'Simon', a nine-year-old boy who 'finds schoolwork boring and seldom participates in classroom activities. Through establishing a well-planned multimodal learning environment based on digital storytelling which allowed Simon to experience making, drawing, painting, taking photos, music and communication, the child became interested and motivated and produced his own digital stories. Interestingly Nilsson then asks: 'Is Simon literate?' She explicates with:

> If literacy is limited to forming and decoding letters then Simon is not. If understanding literacy as a social and cultural activity where semiotic means of different kinds are used for producing texts in processes of expressing and creating meaning and communicating, then Simon is highly literate. (Nilsson 2010, p. 9)

The message is that 'writing in a monomodal manner was not possible for Simon and that reading and writing were obstacles rather than tools for him' (Nilsson 2010, p. 9). Nilsson's research evidence led her to the conclusion that in school, 'learning to write is reduced to conquering a code, the exercise becomes a surface imitation of genres and text-types without being rooted in what is the core of language' (Nilsson 2010, p. 2). Instead of being founded on and around the needs and interests of children as they naturally develop and on their activity,

> writing is given to them from without, from the teacher's hands. This situation recalls the development of a technical skill such as piano playing: the pupil develops finger dexterity and learns to strike the keys while reading music, but he is in no way involved in the essence of the music itself. (Vygotsky 1978, p. 117)

These theories have been supported by a range of strategies which reinforce the monomodal model, for example print-based word lists. Critical approaches to multiliteracies[1] and multimodality are 'currently conceived as key alternatives to addressing failures in traditional language reading pedagogies in preparing pupils for interactions in the cross-cultural and technologised world' (Hibbert 2009, p. 204). Each child who enters a classroom comes from a context, an environment, a world in which 's/he is surrounded by multimodality' (Kress et al. 2001). The contrast in experience and the reduction of pedagogy from multi to mono is 'likely to alienate young people and may diminish the development of their full scholastic potential' (Hibbert 2009, p. 204). 'Literacy in educational contexts is most often approached as a motor skill and not as a complex social, cultural and creative activity' (Nilsson 2010, p. 2).

Although we advocate the use of multimodality in its empirical definition to support learning we are aware of the potential limitations to knowledge construction related to digital multimodality. The replacement of narrative knowledge-based teaching by digital technology is a flawed paradigm because of its assumption of a 'one-size-fits-all' undifferentiated pedagogy (Alexander 2004), and an over-reliance on technology. Ohler (2007) makes the point that 'the problem for many students is their focus on the power of the technology rather than the power of their stories. Some students are engaging the medium at the expense of the message, producing a technical event rather than a story' (Ohler 2007, p. 45). To develop children as communicators, literacy teaching needs to be re-thought and teachers need to 'renegotiate its general objectives' (Katsarou & Tsafos 2010, p. 50).

> A school that prepares students for the contemporary dynamic communication landscape by using multimodal approaches to learning, turns its students into active producers and readers/listeners of multimodal texts in a manner that will allow them to become critically literate through understanding that a text is not a transparent window on reality but is constructed. (Katsarou & Tsafos 2010, p. 50)

This strategy based on the active involvement of the learner in his/her own learning (Perrenoud 1998) will enable those students to 'develop agency as a communicator rather than opting for media-promoted passivity' (Dufflemeyer & Ellertson 2005, in Katsarou & Tsafos 2010, p. 50). Our research in actively involving 'James' in his own learning through his immersion into the genre of fairytales is essentially rooted in that philosophy. We advocate that teachers adopt a balanced pedagogy between the exposure of the child to traditional books set against the modern over-reliance and dominance of technological

---

[1]In Multiliteracies the New London Group (2000, p. 9) argues that literacy pedagogy now must account for the burgeoning variety of text forms associated with information and multimedia technologies.

resources. The recent history of educational systems (e.g. international test score comparisons, league tables, e-testing, minimum competency standards measurement on accountancy models, etc.) has shown that the failure to involve pupils as active producers and participants in learning results in a model which is negative, that is, prescribed and standardised styles of pedagogy and assessment, reduced curriculum breadth and experiences.

Methodology

To evidence the possibilities of using a multimodal teaching strategy for developing the communication skills through the storytelling of a five-year-old, we focused on the genre of fairytales. 'In most cases personal stories are bland and uninspiring and invite little comment from others. In contrast, the retellings of oral and fairytale stories more often containing literary phrases are accompanied by gesture and sometimes character voices' (Harrett 2002, p. 19). We conducted the following research study in a medium sized (350 pupils) inner city primary school in Liverpool. The focus was on the reception and production of language and the judicious use of multimodal strategies and peer collaboration in supporting the child's storytelling skills over five sessions of 30 minutes each. We had selected three fairytales (Hansel and Gretel, Rapunzel, The Frog Prince) to use over the five sessions. Five separately sourced illustrations for each of the three fairytales were selected to use as an integral part of the conversations with the child. We were mindful of the impact of fairytales on one child's storytelling skills to 'reflect a greater increase in ability to understand and remember stories' (Salvetti 2001, p. 80).

However, the importance of understanding children's stories as conceptual structures, as proposed by Applebee (1978), alongside the recognition of true narrative, must be delineated. Applebee's (1978) study of children's storytelling recognises that there are 'modes of organisation' that make up six major stages of narrative form: 'Heaps, sequences, primitive narratives, unfocused chains, focused chains and true narratives' (p. 72). Of these, Vygotsky's 'heaps' is the least complex in form and is rooted in the child's perception and is essentially unrelated to the characteristics of the material to be organised (p. 57). For example, 'a girl, a boy and a mother and the piggy and then a horse, etc.' (Applebee 1978, p. 72). The 'true narrative' which Vygotsky (1962) describes as 'incidents are (now) linked both by centring and by chaining are thus more fully controlled' (cited in Applebee 1978, p. 69). These stages of development are sequential and there are obvious links of progression to be applied at each stage. However, Applebee recognises the dangers in placing children neatly in each stage and category and argues that 'these can apply recursively' (1978, p. 72). Equally important is the area of narrative structure in children's storytelling. An accepted expectation is for children to have an appropriate beginning, middle and end to their stories.

Teachers need to be conscious of the balance between structure (as above) and that 'such a reception of language allows … greater possibilities of production of language' (Kingman Report 1988, Chapter 2, para. 23).

Limitations of the methodology include the small scale of the study (one child, James, with facilitator/peer, Kwame), negating the generalisability of the conclusions, and the possible 'outsider-researcher' effect of a limited understanding of the child and his learning needs, the sequential steps in that learning and the ability to plan multimodal experiences to match and support that learning. This requires balanced support for the affective and cognitive domains of the child. It demands that teachers have a theoretical construct of learning with the child at the centre rather than a focus on one-size-fits-all methodology and planning (Boyle & Charles 2010a).

We worked with James and the rest of his guided group in a quiet area of the classroom for the sessions. In each of the five sessions, we took observation notes as well as recording the dialogue at each session, and for reliability compared their recorded observations at the end of each of the five sessions. We were looking for clear developments in narrative structure and wanted to move away from the simplistic 'beginning, middle and end' strategy, so we incorporated Gamble and Yates's (2002, p. 39) model of narrative structuring. It is delineated in four ways:

(i)   Exposition (the scene is set and characters are introduced);
(ii) Complication (the characters' lives become complicated in some way);
(iii) Climax (this is the point in the story where suspense is at its highest);
(iv) Resolution (provides a solution for the complication – though this is not necessarily a happy one).

After an initial discussion with James, an enthusiastic child but a reticent contributor to whole-class oral discussions, a summer-born five-year-old (see Sykes et al. (2009) for negative performance effects on summer-born children), we decided to work with him. The initial conversation focused on James's awareness of fairytales and it suggested that he had had no exposure to them and was reluctant about revealing the depth of his knowledge. When asked: 'Do you know the story called Hansel and Gretel?' James replied 'No'. 'Have you heard the story about a girl called Cinderella?'; James's reply, 'No'. 'What about another girl with very long hair called Rapunzel?'; James's reply, 'No'. It was noted that continuing with the questions may have caused James to feel inadequate so the questions were stopped. James's response reflects Williams's (1991) comment on the danger of expecting children to respond to text in a certain way: with 'Personal responses as though they were universal features of childhood' (in Hunt 1999, p. 157). The opposite actually applies and 'it is crucial that teachers recognise that initial engagement with a text is usually a private event' (Vandergrift 1995, p. 1), allowing children time and opportunities for reflection and assimilation.

At the beginning of the study we investigated James's current storytelling ability by conducting two baseline exercises. To aid his storytelling in the baseline exercise, the only prompts used were 'tell me the story of ...', 'how did the story start?' and 'who was in the story?'. The baseline was established through recording and transcribing James's version of the story of 'Spot the Dog'. He was shown only the front cover of the story book and then asked to tell the story. He said:

'He hides, he looks for his mum, he is in the basket.'

The following day James was shown the cover of 'Where's my bear?' Again he was asked to tell the story. He said:

'The big bear is in the woods, and the little boy is frightened, then they go home.'

Research sessions

The first session involved the author reading the Hansel and Gretel fairytale to James. This took, with actions and showing the book's illustrations, about 15 minutes. James at the conclusion of the fairytale asked spontaneously 'Can we read that again?' We read the fairytale again. This desire to hear the story again indicates a real sense of enjoyment of fairytales from James (Marriott 1991, p. 9). Sénéchal's research evidences the enhanced impact on young children of expressive language in fairytales' (in Saracho & Spodek 2002, p. 64). Further, McKeown (2001) "discusses the importance of 'aural comprehension' and argues that 'this ability is usually very high in children' (p. 10). Gamble and Yates (2002) recognise that 'understanding of a written text is much higher when it is read aloud by a skilled reader' (p. 122). After the re-reading of Hansel and Gretel, James wanted to look more closely at the illustrations in the book to re-establish in his mind who the characters were.

Vandergrift's observation that 'initial engagement with a text is usually a private event' (Vandergrift 1995, p. 1) is reflected in James's reaction to this sequence from session one. James commented on the characters: 'She's a horrible mum and there's the witch'. However, when we then asked James to 'tell me the story of Hansel and Gretel', James replied: 'I don't know it', thereby confining his thoughts to himself on this 'private event'. Consider a Year 1 (aged 5–6) classroom in which the teacher was reading the story 'Abiyoyo'. After the part of the story in which Abiyoyo is introduced as 'a giant called Abiyoyo as tall as a tree and he could eat people up', the teacher asked 'who is Abiyoyo?' Her intent was that the children describe Abiyoyo and why people fear him – because he eats people. However, in the excerpt below it is clear that children do not get very far into these ideas.

The discussion that ensued after the teacher's initial question of 'Who is Abiyoyo?' follows:

Child S: A monster.

Teacher: Did the story say he was a monster?

S: It's a big green man.

T: A big green man. But does the story say what the big green man was?

S: He is tall.

S: A giant.

T: He is a giant and he is as tall as a ----.

Class: Tree.

T: Tree. OK so what is this all about?

S: Monsters.

T: What is this story all about?

S: Giant.

(Beck & McKeown 2001, p. 15)

Here is another example of what starts out as a monosyllabic response to personal storytelling in the context of a theme on personal histories and the development of that storytelling through a multimodal intervention (audio-tape):

First version: 'I just feel … pop … that's all'.

but when the child listens to himself and his peers telling stories he produces 33 words as follows:

Second version: 'I been to the park after that I play swing then I play slides with my sister then after that I play football after football I been swimming after swimming I been home'. (Harrett 2002, p. 21)

The monosyllabic responses of the children viewed within a socio-linguistic perspective, it could be argued, are all that could be expected. Surely it also indicates that this is what the children are used to contributing. Possibly this is all the teacher anticipates receiving from the child and, within the limits of time allowed in her plan, all that she really wants. The teacher's pedagogy has created a learning environment of discrete entities, that is, 'text', 'knowledge', 'teacher' and 'child/learner' leading to 'children's own knowledge and experiences in this situation having to defer to the status conferred by the teacher on text features' (Kirby 1996, p. 9). This leads to the children being forced to play a continual guessing game of 'what is in the teacher's head?' Kirby's research also evidenced that 'the teachers began to understand in a deeper way the difficulties children faced when asked to respond to de-contextualised language, as much as the language may have appeared explicit to us as adult readers'

Figures 3.1–3.5   The Hansel and Gretel story

(1996, p. 16). Whole-class scenarios can be unrealistic arenas to enable children to develop as storytellers because the teacher imposes demands of pace and coverage in place of reflection and measured shared composition.

Session one only contained one storytelling episode as we were concerned about cognitive overload (Graves 1994) because of James's age and a desire to nurture his affective domain development: 'Affect is a student's internal belief system' (Tait-McCutcheon 2008, p. 507).

The second session, the following week, began with recapping the previous storytelling session. We asked James 'What was the story called that I read to you last time?'

James said: 'The Gingerbread Man'. In using these words instead of the title of the story (Hansel and Gretel), James appeared to be making an inter-textual link, but at the expense of omitting the central characters' names and the title of the story, because the house to which the witch takes the children is made of gingerbread.

James then retold the Hansel and Gretel story in more detail: 'The lady put a boy in a cave, the girl was going in a [sic] oven, they went to bed'.

The pattern of the research was to show pictures to structure the story retelling in each of the sessions. James was shown five pictures, one at a time, to stimulate his narrative recall of the story (Figures 3.1–3.5).

This multimodal structuring to his storytelling ability (see below) produced a much richer version of the story from James:

> Once upon a time the boy and the girl went to bed, the mum was in the forest, then they came back home, then they seen [sic] the gingerbread house and the witch locked them in the cave, they found the treasure. They brought them back to the dad.

The use of illustrations develops and extends James's storytelling skills within the multimodal linking of thinking, images and visual connections (Zitlow 2000). Sénéchal et al. state that 'intervention studies using picture books have shown positive effects in pre-school children's narrative production based on books and pictures' (2008, p. 42). However, a note of caution is sounded by Beck and McKeown (2001) in that 'children can ignore the linguistic content and respond just from the visual' and meaning can be compromised when 'the pictures are in conflict with what is going on in the text' (p. 15). However, Beck and McKeown qualify this comment and state that he has observed teachers using pictures judiciously and timing their inclusion. This produced responses that were linked directly to the text being read. It is here that strategising judiciously plays a key role in developing children's responses, especially if we consider how young children develop. Many four- and five-year-olds would effectively 'switch off' when listening to a story if the pictures were not available. Zitlow (2000) reminds us that we all think and learn by using images.

At the end of the session, James was read a new fairytale called 'Rapunzel'. He made a repeated request for 'Can we read that again?'

On the third session, in response to a request to retell Rapunzel, James appeared somewhat reluctant to engage with the story as a whole. The use of illustrations did not enable James to elaborate the narrative structures of Rapunzel. For example, James's reductionist version of the story was: 'A witch cuts the girl's hair off, the end.'

James was asked 'Who else is in this story?' He replied 'I don't know'.

Authors: Where did the witch put Rapunzel to live?

James: I don't know.

We reflected on our observations of James in this third session. Following the principle of allowing children time and opportunities for reflection and assimilation, teachers should be able to recognise that 'initial engagement with a text is usually a private event' (Vandergrift 1995, p. 1). As Fenwick observes (1990, p. 54) 'children's responses are like an iceberg, nine tenths of which is submerged beneath the surface'. By implication, some teachers' expectations can either shut down or open up possibilities for response (Carey et al. 1996, p. 133). It is important that teachers should scaffold (Bruner 1983) the discussion in order for children to learn the nature of narrative, and thereby facilitate their participation (Salvetti 2001, p. 77). In short, children see through quiz-like questions and produce limited responses that consequently lead those teachers to perceive that the child's insight is limited. Similarly, Marriott (1995) argues that '"Why" questions, children find very difficult to answer and to explain reasons for a particular judgement is a very sophisticated skill (higher order)' (p. 92). The researchers discussed the way forward after a session in which James appeared to have 'stood still'. One route was to introduce James to visual literacy (drawings, illustrations) to stimulate his interest in storytelling and its linguistic content (QCA 2004, p. 4). Beck and McKeown support the view that 'children can more readily derive information from pictures in comparison to text language' (2001, p. 11). However, the decision was made to introduce a more orally capable peer to the group in session 4 for the 'social mediation of knowledge' (Vygotsky 1978), that is, supporting James through his zone of proximal development. 'By interacting with a peer who tells stories in a developmentally more advanced form than the child, the child enters his/her zone of proximal development' (Vygotsky 1978, in Cassell et al. 2002). Sometimes the multimodal strategy needs a socially mediated support element – in this case, we determined on peer collaboration as the additional variable.

At the end of session 3, James was read a new story, 'The Frog Prince'.

For session 4, we introduced a more capable peer (Kwame) and at the start of the session asked James to retell the story of Hansel and Gretel for Kwame:

'James, Kwame does not know the story of Hansel and Gretel. Please tell it to him and use the pictures to help you'.

James said:

> Once upon a time there was a little girl and a little boy, they left their house, then they saw the gingerbread house, the witch locked them in a cave. "I'm going to eat you." She put the girl in the oven and they found the treasure and went home to daddy.

James, who had been read the Hansel and Gretel story in session 2, i.e. two weeks ago, had internalised that story and was able to recount it to Kwame without textual support from the teacher.

In comparing James's storytelling in session 1 and now in session 4, the inclusion of character speech indicates a deeper understanding of the story and characterisation. The increase in vocabulary and evidence of audience awareness is noteworthy. This corresponds with the effects of peer collaboration in storytelling in Jordan, Snow and Porche's research (2000, in Saracho & Spodek 2002, p. 82) which indicates 'a moderate effect on vocabulary, story comprehension and story sequence'.

In this session James is encouraged to retell Rapunzel's narrative to Kwame. James demonstrates both willingness and excitement as he talks:

> The witch cut the girl's hair off. Let down your golden hair, the girl married the prince.

It is significant that as this is James's second retelling event in this session, the cognitive burden (Graves 1994) is being demonstrated by the reduced nature of his narrative output. However, we note how James inserts distinct phrases within his storytelling, as in Hansel and Gretel. This is particularly significant when one recalls James's previous lack of participation without the direct involvement of a collaborator. This again signals the importance of peer collaboration as proposed by Vygotsky (1978) and Cassell et al. (2002). As a cautionary note it must be remembered that James (any child) will not produce full versions of a story on every occasion as there are limitations to peer collaboration even within group situations.

At the end of this session (session 4), both James and Kwame were read 'The Frog Prince'.

At the beginning of the fifth session James was asked to retell the Frog Prince story from last week's session. James continued to take the initiative as he had in the last session and commenced a sequence of questions for Kwame about the Frog Prince as follows: Do you know the prince? Do you know the golden ball? Do you know the king? The water and the pond? Here James is probing Kwame's awareness of the story, utilising the same structure of questioning which we had used with him initially.

James continued but in narrative rather than questioning mode:

'The frog came in and jumped on the table and ate the dinner.' 'Open the door and let the frog in.' 'I am tired, I want to sleep on the pillow.' The wicked witch turned the prince into a frog.

Here James is demonstrating characteristics of three stages of Applebee's modes of organisation of storytelling, that is sequences, primitive narratives and unfocused chains (Applebee 1978) and is including more direct character speech, in this instance three direct quotations from the story. Ryokai et al.'s research (2003) evidenced that children who played with a virtual peer used more quoted speech and temporal and spatial expressions (p. 195).

Kwame, having retained the initial questions from James, now had space to respond and asked: 'What happened to the ball?' James replied 'The princess threw the ball high in the sky and then it fell into the pond'. This example of true collaboration and the dialogic process in action (Wells 2001b; Boyle & Charles 2010a) demonstrates the potential for supporting the internalisation of narrative communication. This is further demonstrated as the two boys continue in the session and James starts, unprompted, to retell the Rapunzel story to Kwame. It would seem that James has now engaged with storytelling as a process which he wants to share with his peer.

James:	Once upon a time Rapunzel's mum and dad went in the witch's garden and then she caught Rapunzel's dad. 'Go and get Rapunzel' Rapunzel went up the ladder.
Kwame interrupts:	No it was the witch who goes down the ladder.
James:	'Rapunzel, Rapunzel, let down your golden hair.' Then they got married and the witch died.

It is interesting that James chooses to ignore Kwame's correction and hastily concludes the story. The whole exchange in this session between James and Kwame exemplifies the dialogic process as outlined in Wells (2001b). It is also significant that James and Kwame did not need an intervention from us at this stage to stimulate their storytelling.

Conclusion

This small-scale research study focused on a limited investigation of the impact of fairytales on one child's storytelling skills in multimodal and multiliteracy contexts, in this case the integration of speaking, listening and reading. Salvetti (2001) reminds the reader that the impact of fairytales on children's storytelling skills 'reflects a greater increase in their ability to understand and remember stories' (Salvetti 2001, p. 80). Gamble and Yates (2002) strongly correlate children's understanding of written texts as much higher when read aloud by a skilled reader (p. 122).

The implications of failing to acknowledge and implement the importance of time and silence are evidenced in the first storytelling session. It is accepted that this one example cannot claim to be conclusive, but a response from James of 'I don't know', immediately after he has listened to a story, strongly suggests his need for time and reflection (Fenwick 1990; Vandergrift 1995). Teachers need to be cognisant of the importance of children being given time for immersion and reflection as a means of deepening their responses to story situations. Wells (1984) cautions avoidance of intervening or supplying solutions or meanings far too quickly (cited in Jones 1988, p. 56).

The comparative results of James's sessions are significant. A range of modalities are strategically introduced and incorporated. Illustrations are introduced in session 2 and continue to be used throughout each of the sessions. Their inclusion allied to other modalities (talking with Kwame, listening to the story, action and movement by the storyteller, dramatic story sound effects) support and scaffold a significant improvement of James's storytelling skills from his efforts in his baseline and first session. Using a synthesis of Gamble and Yates's (2002) narrative model and Applebee's six major stages of narrative form, James progressed from being initially located at the 'heaps' stage to demonstrating evidence of moving towards more developed stages of narrative form (Applebee 1978). James's movement in and out of the development stages without being 'rooted' or located firmly in one stage demonstrates the fluidity and progressive nature of linguistic development.

A natural extension in strategy for James and Kwame to progress further would be working in a guided group situation. This would enable 'an organisational approach where attention can be given to particular children who may require additional support or challenge to ensure that they continue to progress' (Williams 2008, p. 67). However, we would attach a caveat to Williams's definition: the guided group strategy should not be misconstrued as a group of children requiring special needs support. The opposite, in fact, is true – a guided group is the optimal teaching, learning and assessment situation in which the lead professional in the classroom is focused on the individual(s) learning support.

CHAPTER 4

USING BIG BOOKS AS VISUAL LITERACIES TO SUPPORT EMERGENT WRITERS

Introduction

This chapter focuses on a group of 'beginning readers' and the strategies being used by their teacher to deepen their understandings of the text being read aloud to them and with the children reading aloud themselves. The dominant strategy was a multimodal use of paintings and penned illustrations to create and author their own books. Through using a core reading scheme (Oxford Reading Tree) the children were also encouraged to 'behave' as readers through taking part in writing self-generated sentences and the associated learning behaviours from the teacher modelling in small guided groups, such as re-reading their sentences to gain awareness of overall coherence, syntax and spelling strategies. In addition, we incorporated a device of visualising techniques and visual representation within a three levelled structure: 'Before reading', students visually organise their thinking, visualising the possible content linking background knowledge and forming predictions. 'During reading', students visualise the content, comparing predictions with ideas, themes and information in the text. They begin to form a visual representation of what they are reading. And finally, 'after reading, students visually link new information with prior knowledge, visually represent what they have read in a graphic summary and build new understandings' (Draper 2012, p. 2). According to Gambrell and Jawitz (1993), 'if we combine the ability to generate mental imagery (visualisation) and the integration and use of multimodalities provided in a text, there is greater effect on understanding the material and enhanced comprehension' (p. 266). However, when text illustrations do not match the story, comprehension can decrease and learning can be reduced. One way to overcome this obstacle is to allow the students to become engaged in the story and critique the illustrations after analysis of the text Nielsen (Hibbing & Rankin-Erickson 2003, p. 763). This also raises important pedagogical implications linked to the concept of dual coding (Clark & Paivio 1991) or the coding of knowledge in both verbal and non-verbal representations. In Hibbing et al.'s study (2003), the researchers observed that children with whom they had worked did not automatically create images, or were not able to do so with conscious effort. Rather than creating images located with meaning, many of them focused on the decoding of words, for instance when asked about the reading which they had just completed, Shaun (pseudonym) said: 'I don't know what happened, I was too busy reading the words' (p. 759). In contrast, some students 'read the words fluently but still lacked the ability to create mental images that related to the text … putting comprehension at risk' (Nielsen-Hibbing et al. 2003, p. 759). Although reading and writing are complementary skills whose development runs a roughly parallel course, they do not go hand in hand, 'while readers form a mental representation of thoughts written by someone else, writers formulate their own thoughts, organise them, and create a written record of them using the conventions of spelling and grammar' (Graham & Perin 2007, pp. 7–8). However, our leading principle – is that reading and writing are both communication activities and writers should gain insight about reading by creating their own texts (Tierney & Shanahan 1991), leading to better comprehension of texts produced by others (Graham & Hebert 2010, p. 12) – guided our work, and even though writing development was the main component it was contextualised within a core literacy paradigm of speaking, listening and reading.

What is visual literacy?

We see the concept of visual literacy as emerging in the late 1960s from the ideas of the prominent writer, John Debes (1968). According to Debes:

> visual literacy is the name given to a couple of visual efficiencies that are developed by the individual's utilisation of visual sensation. The development of these efficiencies is the basis for learning. The individual who possesses these has the improved skills for discriminating and interpreting visual motions, objects, symbols and other things in the environment. By creatively using these efficiencies, the individual communicates with other people and uses visual communication more effectively. (1968, p. 961)

Ausburn and Ausburn (1978) states that 'visual literacy is what is seen with the eye and what is seen with the mind' (p. 291). While Bamford (2003) reports that a visually literate person should 'be able to read and write visual language and this includes the ability to successfully decode (read) and interpret visual messages and to encode (write) and compose meaningful visual communications' (p. 1). A commissioned report on behalf of the National Council for Curriculum and Assessment by Kennedy et al. (2012) built on a broad conceptualisation of the early work of Debes and recognises the importance of multiple modes and representations in literacy. It also defines literacy from a semiotic position to include linguistic and non-linguistic forms of communication (NCCA 2012 p. 54). By shifting from the singular literacy, that is simple decoding, to the recognition of plural literacies, this concept of enlarged reading escapes the narrow confines of the printed text to encompass a wide range of cultural, technological and visual elements (Williams 2007, p. 636).

There are many forms of visual communication, including gestures, objects, signs and symbols. Visual signs are everywhere, for example, dance, film, fashion, hair styles, exhibitions, public monuments, interior design, lighting, computer games, advertising, photography, architecture and art are just some examples of visual communication. To be visually literate, a person should be able to understand the subject matter of images and:

- analyse the syntax of images including style and composition;
- analyse the techniques used to produce the image;
- evaluate the aesthetic merit of the work;
- evaluate the merit of the work in terms of purpose and audience;
- understand the synergy, interaction, innovation, affective impact and/or 'feel' of an image. (Bamford 2003, p. 1)

A simple example of the above statement, 'analyse the syntax of images including style and composition', is supplied in the vignette from Callow's (2008) study on the 'principles for assessing visual literacy' as follows:

> Have you ever learned something about looking up and down? Jay asked me as we read a picture book in his classroom. His third grade teacher had recently been incorporating a discussion of pictures and visual texts into her teaching. 'The person that looks down is the strongest one' he informed me, referring to the concept of a low angle where the viewer is positioned looking up to a character in a picture, making them appear stronger and more powerful'. 'That is really good information and what about the person looking up?' I asked. 'She is terrified', Jay responded, clearly imagining a weaker image in a situation where the viewer is located above a character who is then looking up to them. (Callow 2008, p. 616)

This emphasises to us that images are not simply illustrating the text nor are they decorations – images are their own system of meaning and we need to teach children how to read images as well as text (Draper 2012, p. 14).

Let us now consider how visual literacy (through the methodology of the Show Me framework) is used in a classroom setting.

The Show Me framework is an Australian initiative and consists of three dimensions located within the teaching of visual literacy. These three dimensions are: the affective, the compositional and the critical.

The affective dimension is an expression of enjoyment when examining images or exploring pictures as signs of affective engagement. These may also be assessed by observation of facial features and gestures, the engaged discussions about a picture and the evident pleasure taken as children partake in an activity. The affective also involves personal interpretation where viewers bring their own experiences and aesthetic preferences to an image (Callow 2008, p. 618).

The compositional dimension is the use of specific meta-language and is the key to this dimension. Concepts such as actions, symbols, shot-length, angles, gaze, colour, layout, salience, lines and vectors reflect a meta-linguistic knowledge about visual texts. These same concepts may also be present in longer less linguistically succinct terms, where a child talks about objects on a page because they are large or bright (salience). Teachers would need to know the concepts and related meta-language when listening for such comments in an assessment context (Callow 2008, p. 618).

The critical dimension is the assessment of socio-critical understandings and will vary depending on the text and learning situation. For younger students comments about how the illustrator did not draw the scene clearly or effectively might be precursors to more complex critiques of choices made in illustrations. Older students may be using more specific comments, such as talking about how an image positions the viewer to think or feel in a particular way. Although each aspect of visuality is important, ideological critique is perhaps the most challenging for students and teachers (Callow 2008, p. 618).

The Show Me dimensions in practice (with pupils aged 7–8)

The students described in our introductory vignette had been exploring visual literacy where visual texts from picture books, information books and video were not only used for content, but also specific visual aspects were explored. During one week, the picture books of Anthony Browne were used as part of the read-aloud and shared reading sessions. While reading the book *Gorilla* (Browne 2000), the teacher pointed out how some pictures attract attention by their use of colour, size or angles. Working in pairs with their own copy of the book, the students were encouraged to find one picture that they found curious or interesting, place a small sticky note on it, and then describe to each other what specific feature they thought made it interesting. The class also completed drawings and labelling activities while further extending discussion around the visual images in more of Browne's books.

In terms of the affective dimension, the teacher had noted that all students enthusiastically talked about and discussed the picture books during the week. On an individual basis each child was able to comment on a favourite page from *Willy and Hugh* (Browne 1998), giving reasons why they each liked their chosen picture. Focusing on the compositional aspects of expression, size and angle, Buster Nose (the bully of the story) was discussed with each child who was able to explain why he/she thought that Buster looked powerful. Some said 'his face is really big' and 'he takes up the whole room', while others commented on his expression and clothes, 'his mouth is angry' and 'his outfit has all spikes on it'. Jay, from our opening quote, was the most articulate from his new-found knowledge about angles. He explained 'he is bigger and he is taking up more of the page and he is looking down. I can tell that because there's glasses on at an angle'. When questioned about a symbolic picture of the two main characters shaking hands (with just the hands shown in close-up suggesting friendship) no child interpreted this as showing care, friendship or kindness. Rather they all gave a literal description that they were just 'shaking hands'. The critical dimension proved the weakest for these students, with most having limited responses about why they thought that Browne might have written the book or what the theme might be. They gave short comments such as 'being nice' or 'be friendly to others', while some commented on a specific event in the book such as 'if you accidentally knock someone over you can be nice to them' rather than a broader theme or idea (Callow 2008, pp. 620–622).

This classroom example illustrates a majority of the Show Me principles, in that it is part of authentic, contextualised learning in a class; it involves formative assessment and provides varied means for students to show their skills and use authentic texts while providing focused assessment activities involving specific meta-language as part of the overall assessment process.

The complexity of visual literacy

Teachers need to understand both the complex yet simple nature of visual literacy. For example, in Williams's (2007) study of 'reading the painting' she recalls an episode in which a teacher assumes that the student has the skill set required to interpret meaning from a painting:

Teacher: 'Carrie, look at the painting. What do you see? What story do you see?'

Student: 'Well, there is a guy on a bench and he is reading something'.

Teacher: 'Who is the guy? Why is he sitting on a bench? Read me the story in the painting.'

Student: (puzzled expression on her face): 'How am I supposed to do that? There aren't any words there.' (Williams 2007, p. 636).

For children to be supported by teachers' understanding of and therefore use of visual literacy, visual literacy has to be recognised officially and its status enshrined in national curricula internationally. This will then scaffold teachers towards a deeper concept of their own supportive pedagogy, a pedagogy embedded in authentic contextualised activities rather than the current classroom orthodoxy of binary, decoding activities for easy marking and grading purposes. Our own classroom observations confirm the opposite of teachers' understandings incorporating enlarged definitions of literacy in which visual modes are explored by the children in rich and motivating ways. Instead, we have observed children in relatively large groups (12–17) sitting passively receiving instruction after instruction on print-based lessons (i.e. phonics). Very rarely have we observed a conceptual distancing from text to other semiotic modes. In the lessons we observed there was an urgent need for teachers to understand a multi-modal use of literacy. In short, no lessons ever originated or had as their starting point an illustration which had the potential to develop into other forms of meaning; instead, we observed the teacher/teaching assistant covering up images/illustrations and asking the children to focus on the printed text for meaning. There were similar findings, in a recent study by Moyles and Worthington (2011) across eight authorities throughout England, in which 10 reception classes were studied by seven different observers. The research data demonstrated that teacher-led literacy showed little in terms of meaningful contexts for children, rather a great amount of time spent on synthetic phonics. Of the total time children engaged in literacy, 33.6 per cent was spent on listening to the teacher read a story, 39.4 per cent on phonics and only 12.6 per cent on reading (Moyles Worthington 2011, p. 3). Similarly, there was an apparent lack of breadth in the curriculum and little opportunity for collaborative and sustained dialogue with adults and/or peers, important for children's language and cognitive development. In teacher-led activities, teachers generally gave children very precise (closed) instructions and resources that meant that there were few opportunities for children to use their own ideas and very little adult interaction to support and develop children's ideas (Moyles & Worthington 2011, p. 3). The study went on to conclude with many salient recommendations, one of which viewed the teacher's role as one of critical engagement with theory and continued reading of classroom and pedagogical literature. It seems from this study that narrow assessment emphasis and an excess of initiatives and curriculum changes have mainly failed to allow for the development of open-ended pedagogies responsive to the child. Sustained, complex and challenging learning can only come through teachers' higher-level understanding of children's day-to-day curriculum experiences translated into effective pedagogy (p. 4). Williams (2007) evidenced through her small-scale study that 'despite building background knowledge with an author study, for example Quentin Blake's picture books, and despite the modelling and think-alouds on his paintings (composition and perspective, colour, tone, vocabulary) many of the pairs of children had a difficult time getting started with this alternative approach to reading comprehension, that is, visual literacy.

> With their first painting I found that many were simply 'describing' the picture, not looking at it narratively. For example, one team wrote 'There is a man. He's standing on a bridge. It is night. There are lots of stars.'

> This type of descriptive response was not unlike what they had done in other writing until that point. The children were providing a literal written re-translation of the painting, devoid of any subjective or unique interpretations. (Williams 2007, p. 638)

Here Williams is clearly identifying the necessarily complex nature of learning to read a visual. However, we feel that this is an example of the stepped process that happens regularly during children's learning journeys, for example the incremental transition from concrete to abstract thinking. So Williams regrouped and adopted questioning strategies traditionally used with printed texts (Beck & McKeown 1996; Keene & Zimmerman 1997) and because the students were already familiar with 'Questioning the Author' technique, this was modified to 'Questioning the Painter'. The following example reflects how two students used the simplified KWL Strategy (K-W-L is a group activity developed by Donna Ogle (1986) that helps students think actively while reading. K--- teachers activate students' prior knowledge by asking them what they KNOW about a topic; W--- helping students determine what they WANT to know or learn; L--- students identify what they LEARN as they read) (Ogle 1986). The students were shown *The Double Jockey Act* by Jack B. Yeats, which depicts a darkly lit circus, where two men perform a double jockey trick on horseback as a clown runs alongside them (see the painting on the National Gallery of Ireland website, at http://www.nationalgallery.ie/en/aboutus/Images_and_Licensing/Print_Sales/Yeats_Collection/The_Double_Jockey_Act.aspx).

First the students used bullets to record what they knew based on observations from the painting. Then they took these 'facts' and incorporated them into their narrative:

> One dark night when the kiyotys [coyotes] were howling, there was a circus. At the circus two men were riding a horse doing tricks. The two men were fauther [father] and son. The fauthers name was Jack and the son was Joe. And the clown that was pretending to be a horse his name was Osi. The circus was in canada. As Mr. Jack and Joe did there tricks the audience claped. Then all of suden two men from the audience went to the ecwetment tent and stole all of the ecwetment [equipment]. But then the clown saved the day and put them in jail. And he saved the day and they lived happily ever after the End. (Williams 2007, p. 639)

Visual literacy and writing

A report by Graham and Hebert (2010) entitled *Writing to Read* listed as number one in their recommendations of closely related instructional practices shown to be effective in improving children's reading as: 'have students write about the texts they read' (p. 13).

> So comprehending a text actively involves creating meaning by building relationships among ideas, building ideas in text and between the text and one's knowledge, beliefs and experiences. Having students write about a text should enhance reading comprehension because it affords greater opportunities to think about ideas in a text, requires them to organise and integrate those ideas into a coherent whole; fosters explicitness, facilitates reflection, encourages personal involvement with texts and involves students transforming ideas into their own words. (Graham & Hebert 2010, p. 21)

This research about writing indicates that there is a need for purposeful writing, writing which motivates, is relevant, purposeful and has an audience. Good practitioners should be developing approaches to engage and motivate learners' writing. Smagorinsky and O'Donnell-Allen (2000) suggest that artwork should facilitate the writing process, resulting in a text that is richer in detail and more intricate than the most traditional writing-first, crayon-drawing-second approach. Millard and Marsh (2001) trace a low esteem for visual literacy by suggesting that 'teachers largely regard the movement from pictures to words as one of intellectual progression' (p. 55). This assumes that drawing is reduced to a stage that children will eventually discard as their writing becomes more sophisticated. Millard and Marsh (2001) also found that 'children appeared to use drawings in an integral way in their written work and there was a strong dialogic relationship between word and image. Differences were found between groups of children who drew before their writing and those that did not, in a study by Norris and Kouider (1998). They found that 'drawing became an effective planning strategy … as a reference point to prompt them towards what should come next in their writing' (1998, p. 71). Ernst (1994) states that, 'the relationship between seeing, telling, drawing, and writing, is intimate, essential and a significant aspect of teaching the writing act' (p. 176). The visual representations by Reception (Kindergarten) children shown in Figures 4.1–4.6 depict the importance of their visual mode playing the leading role in the origination of text for emergent writers. Their images are not simply illustrating the text nor are they decorations, they are their own system of meaning.

Figure 4.1 (Susan) 'I am playing on my own'

Figure 4.2 (Joseph) 'I am playing with my ball'

Figure 4.3   (Jessica) 'I am going to jump in the puddle'

Figure 4.4   (Katie) 'I am playing with my Barbie'

Figure 4.5   (Ryan) 'I am a wrestler'

Figure 4.6   (Jamie) 'I am Spiderman'

Using 'The Show Me dimensions' and 'visualising techniques' in practice (with pupils aged 4–5)

We utilised a two-pronged approach which initially incorporated Draper's (2012) visualising device within a three levelled structure: 'before reading' the children visually organised their thinking, visualising the possible content, linking background knowledge and forming predictions; 'during reading', the children were encouraged to visualise the content, comparing predictions with ideas, themes and information in the text; and finally 'after reading', the children visually linked new information with prior knowledge, visually represented what they had read in a graphic summary and built new understandings' (p. 2). The final strategy incorporated aspects of 'The Show Me dimensions' (Callow 2008) in which the children had been exploring visual literacy where visual texts from picture books, information books and stories were not only used for content, but visual aspects were also explored. During one week, adventure stories from Oxford Reading Tree were used as part of the read-aloud and shared reading sessions. The class teacher also incorporated an exploration of how colour, size, position and angle usage can influence attention and give different meanings to the pictures, and modelled specific language in the guided group sessions using visuals from Roald Dahl and Spike Milligan. The children were encouraged to work in pairs, select a picture each that they had found interesting and describe it to the group.

Conclusion

The chapter detailed opportunities for teachers to focus on integrating writing, illustrations and comprehension strategies. For example, focusing on pacing and allowing real time for immersion, reflection and absorption of information was uppermost in the planning of these concepts, as the avoidance of 'cognitive and sensory overload' remained a real issue for the children and for the teacher to keep at bay.

CHAPTER 5

HOW A GUIDED GROUP TEACHING STRATEGY CAN SUPPORT EMERGING WRITERS

Introduction

We have worked over a number of years with early years children on strategies to enable enjoyment, development and involvement in the writing process. This chapter relates one such initiative in which a group of five children *collaboratively* develop their 'Rain poems' through multimodal teaching strategies, based around the socio-cognitive apprenticeship model of writing (Englert et al. 2006) and an understanding that writing and learning to write are interdependent competencies (Rijlaarsdam et al. 2008). The diverse range expressed in the children's writing and illustrations exemplifies each individual being enabled to self-regulate their impressions of the weather instead of replaying back to the teacher an imposed model 'from without' (Perrenoud 1998; Vygotsky 1978). While detailing the use of the guided group strategy to support writing development, we also explore a model of inclusive group working with a teacher as collaborator and co-constructor (Allal & Ducrey 2000) modelled from the research framework reported in the SPRinG project (Blatchford et al. 2007).

This chapter reports on a mixed ability group of early years children working in a series of lessons to develop their 'Rain poems'. We determined on a mixed ability group composition because 'it is important not to socialise learners into inhibiting views of their own learning and intelligence' (Resnick 2000, p. 1). Tom, the teacher in this study, is early years trained; he has been teaching in the school for approximately 12 years and uses the guided group strategy as a regular teaching method. The school is three form entry and the composition of the class is similar to the two parallel classes in Year 1. The guided group children (Blatchford et al. 2003; Boaler 2005; Boyle & Charles 2012) whose work is exemplified and analysed (to represent for the purposes of this chapter the teacher's normal pedagogy) in this case study were aged four and five years, comprising three boys and two girls from a medium sized (350 pupils) inner city primary school in Liverpool.

The traditional view of grouping for learning in classrooms is that this form of working improves learning but in actuality many of 'these groupings inhibit learning and the motivation to learn' (Blatchford et al. 2007, p. 1). Galton et al. (1980, 1999a and b, 2009) point out that children often spend up to 80 per cent of their classroom time seated in small groups being assigned individual tasks, and the quality of talk within the groups is at a low cognitive level (cited in Blatchford et al. 2007, p. 4). Cowie and Rudduck's (1988) research demonstrated that many children, as well as their teachers, do not like working in groups. Children often feel insecure and threatened when told to work in groups and respond by withdrawal from participation. The SPRinG project (Blatchford et al. 2007) concluded that the main problems identified about group work are 'the limited coordination between the size of groups, the composition, pedagogic purpose of learning tasks and interactions among group members' (p. 5). In summary, the SPRinG data reveal that there is little awareness of social pedagogical relationships or approaches in the group teaching context. The SPRinG report further reveals the limitations in training pupils for effective group work: 'only a quarter of the two hundred teachers in the study reported that they prepared their classes for group working and the majority of these teachers cited "circle time" as their only form of preparation for group work' (Blatchford et al. 2007, p. 6). In the main, the SPRinG data described small groups as likely to be composed of same-sex and same-ability pupils, 'providing contexts of social exclusion rather than inclusion in the classroom' (Blatchford et al. 2007, p. 6). The majority of learning tasks described pupil groups as assigned practice tasks which in fact required children to work alone. Similarly, teacher or adult support was present in 'virtually all of the observations within which new knowledge/cognition was presented to pupils. Therefore, not allowing opportunities for pupils to co-construct and further develop their own new knowledge' (Blatchford et al. 2007, p. 6). A key reported finding of the SPRinG programme and one shared strongly by these authors is that group work skills have to be developed. This case study provides an example of a 'jigsawing' technique in which children take pieces of a theme to form a whole, for example the completion of a group poem.

Goals of a guided group pedagogy

It is important that group learning is not analysed 'independently of the curriculum and the culture of the classroom' and that 'collaborative learning tasks are set up in a way that is conducive to working together and not to independent work' (Blatchford 2007, p. 9). Teachers do need to identify in their planning for group work whether learning tasks are intended to be for collaborative or independent working. For Vygotsky, children learn by solving problems with people more capable than themselves, who take them through their zone of proximal (or potential) development (Vygotsky 1962). Indeed, Vygotsky saw social interaction as *the* essential factor (Smith 1996). In this current research report we stress that teachers need to develop approaches which enable them to explore pupils' thinking and problem-solving strategies by seeking explanations of why the group did certain things in certain ways. This requires an understanding by teachers of the necessary role of socio-cognitive apprenticeships in writing. As part of this developmental process, Englert et al. (2006) discuss the establishment of communities of practice in which pupils 'participate in inquiry-based conversations about texts, learning to treat printed words as thinking devices' (p. 211). When children interact on a frequent basis they have greater opportunity to understand and internalise, 'thereby laying the foundation for the development of dialogical skills that support text production' (Rijlaarsdam et al. 2008, p. 60).

The theoretical underpinning of guided group work is encapsulated in Hayes's (2008) recognition that 'child-centred teaching included behaviour that actively involves children in guiding the learning process, such as offering choices, encouraging activity and suggesting solutions' (p. 433). We propose that teaching 'is not a one way process from the teacher to the child, it is a fluid, dynamic and often seemingly effortless dance between teacher and child' (Matthews 1999, p. 162). Makin and Whiteman (2006) support this view stating that teachers and children 'are partners in teaching and learning transactions. We need to find ways of interacting with children to co-construct shared meanings in ways we cannot do if the children themselves are not active participants in exploring this situation' (p. 35).

Implementing guided group strategy

Our experience of teaching and research in this field has led to an understanding that 'if you are teaching children as a whole class group, rather than planning your teaching and learning around individual learning needs, then you cannot be teaching formatively. If you teach without differentiation then how can you be matching learning to each child's developmental needs?' (Boyle & Charles 2008, p. 22). This has led to a commitment to the principle that group work has to be modelled and understood as teaching and learning through collaboration and co-construction (Allal & Ducrey 2000; Perrenoud 1998) rather than through imposition 'from without' (Vygotsky 1978). Using a guided group strategy in a differentiated classroom 'balances learning needs common to all students with more specific needs tagged to individual learners' (Tomlinson 2001, p. 4). For McAdamis (2001) 'Differentiation allows the teacher to focus on the same key principles for all students, however the instructional process, the pace and rate towards understanding these concepts varies' (p. 3). We define a guided group (Boyle & Charles 2012) as always operating within a whole-class teaching structure, that is, *a movement* from homogeneity to heterogeneity. The guided session will be focused on new learning or on consolidating a concept which the teacher feels that the children have not internalised in their learning, or on pursuing a learning sequence of carefully planned stepped activities. The teacher will have planned for a number of differentiated learning activities within a teaching theme. Three out of the four groups will work independently (or with Teaching Assistant support) on those activities; the fourth group remains with the teacher and continues to be taught – that group is the guided group. The duration of that focused uninter-rupted teaching session for each guided group is around 20 minutes. The teacher plans a rota of guided group sessions to match and challenge the children's learning needs throughout the day and the rest of the week and onwards (Boyle & Charles 2012; Blatchford 2007).

Organisation of guided group strategy

The Williams Report (2008) states that 'Guided group work offers an organ-isational approach where attention can be given to particular children who may require additional support or challenge to ensure they continue to progress in learning' (p. 67). However, we propose a caveat to Williams's definition: the guided group should not be misconstrued as a group requiring special needs support – the opposite in fact. A guided group is the optimal teaching, learn-ing and assessment situation in which the lead professional in the classroom is focused on providing learning support to individual(s). In 2007 the Depart-ment for Children, Schools and Families (DCSF) recognised the importance of these 'organisational and instructional changes' as a move away from the dominance of whole-class teaching – a legacy of the National Literacy and Numeracy Strategies. However, our definition and use of guided group peda-gogy is more systemic and formative than the DCSF's. A guided group teach-ing and assessment session involves the teacher working with a group of no more than five children. Fewer than five children is fine but the group size must enable all the children to collaborate orally. More than five children in the guided group make it difficult for the teacher to carry out the assessment observations and interrogatives which are essential for formative assessment to take place to support learning. The guided group is focused on 'the impor-tance of inquiry, construction and collaboration rather than the delivery of outcomes' (Wells 2001b, p. 2). In the example selected for this chapter, the teacher, Tom, is trying to identify learning misconceptions and to do that he has to facilitate opportunities for all the children in the guided group to demonstrate their learning in an open, equitable and trusting context. Therefore, we agree with Williams's (2008) definition in part but see a guided group offering four things: a strategic (organisational) device; an optimal opportunity for specific and focused teaching; a small-group situation enabling learning to be planned tightly, offering ready accessibility for the child to the teacher; and finally, a rich opportunity for the teacher to focus his/her assessment observations within a maximum group size of five children (Boyle & Charles 2012, p. 123).

Methodology

Working with early years children in the development of their writing skills can be best described in the language of Vygotsky (1962), who defines writing as a separate linguistic function:

> it is speech in thought and image only, lacking the expressive qualities of oral speech. In learning to write, the child must disengage himself from the sensory aspect of speech and replace words by images of words – it is this abstract quality that is the main stumbling block to its use. (p. 181)

Vygotsky reinforces this by underlining that 'writing requires deliberate, analytical work on the part of the children. They put words and sentences together. They must take notice of both the sound structure of words (to get the spelling right) and of word sequences (to get the syntax of sentences right)' (1962, p. 183). In harmony with Vygotsky's conceptualisation is that expressed by Rijlaarsdam et al. (2008). They state that: 'An important phase in learning to write, at all ages, is learning to write by observing and evaluating relevant processes: writing processes, reading processes or communication processes between writers and readers' (Rijlaarsdam et al. 2008, p. 53).

Tom used the strategy of guided group working (grounded in the framework of Blatchford et al. [2007]) to gain an optimal teaching and learning experience for the children (Hayes 2008; Tomlinson 2001). Each group was encouraged to express and develop his/her individual feelings about different types of weather. The teacher planned this unit of work to develop over a number of weeks. Tom's starting point was reading a selection of poetry around the theme of weather to the whole class. He chose poems which enabled him to model descriptive language, common nouns and different types and uses of verbs and prepositions for the group. Tom avoided the socio-educative problems of traditional group work (Blatchford 2007) through developing a classroom culture of respect, collaboration and communication. His pedagogical intentions were always overt, clear and attainable to all the children. Effective group work depends on pupils having the skills to communicate effectively through listening, explaining and sharing ideas and on learning to trust and respect each other (Galton 1990). Baines et al. (2007) argue that 'within the microsystems of a school, there will be social pedagogical sub-systems at the classroom level that have qualitatively distinct sets of relationships, rules and dynamics which can promote or hinder learning and social development' (p. 9).

The children were exposed to and became immersed in poetry for a two-week period. Different types and forms of poems were displayed and read to the children, for example familiar rhymes and thematic poems about 'the weather'. The children then chose their favourite type of weather. Most of the children chose rain and the group decided to write their 'Rain poem'. Each child supplied a line of text and an image to form a complete verse. The complete poem is shown in Figure 5.6. This collaborative process within the guided group can be described as the establishment of 'a socio-cognitive apprenticeship in which teachers and students collaborate, inform, question, think aloud, self-correct, challenge and construct meaning together' (Englert et al. 2006, p. 211). Initially, the sentences were scribed with the children; the teacher made a note of each child's sentence in a notebook. Each child illustrated the rain image which s/he had described in words in their own sentence. Then the sentences were erased from the whiteboard. The children then with different levels of support each wrote out their own sentence. Each child then observed the teacher scribing (modelling) a correct version under his/her own sentence. Finally, each child was encouraged to point to each word in their own sentence as they read it aloud (to encourage one-to-one mapping and the relationship between decoding and encoding of text). The sequence of the above activities enabled each child to have a structure which supported their development as confident experimenters with text. Working within the guided group the children shared their observations and collaborated with ideas freely and over the course of the week the following lines (see following figures) emerged to form a group poem.

Children's poem and analysis

Gary wrote the opening line to the poem, 'Raindrops on cars' (see Figure 5.1). He demonstrates that he understands the use of a specific language style for a line in poem (genre specificity), a very effective short sentence construction. This is a very detailed illustration showing Gary's ownership of content and ideas. The child's illustration in its detail, vividness and completeness demonstrates his enjoyment of the task: note the colours he has chosen and the intricate detail supplied. This is child initiated not teacher imposed. Gary worked on his illustration to demonstrate careful planning and organisation of ideas. We work from the premise that for children 'communication occurs through different but synchronous modes; language, print, images, graphics, movement, gesture, texture, music, and sound' (Kress 2003, p. 51). These synchronous modes form an empirical definition of multimodality, 'a multimodal approach that looks beyond language to all forms of communication' (Jewitt et al. 2009, p. 11). Gary showed a complete connection from concrete (schema) cognition, that is, in his illustration, through to the abstraction of his written representation. Gary is demonstrating that he is beginning to access the complex interactions between media, modes and semiotic resources (Boyle & Charles 2011). Gary is working at the phonemic stage of word construction, demonstrating a good understanding of a partial consonant framework. He represents the beginning and final sounds in the word 'raindrops' (RS). He shows an emerging sight vocabulary developing through the correct usage of 'on'. Careful aural and oral work has enabled Gary to hear all three consonants in the word 'cars'. He also demonstrates an understanding of how to begin a sentence with a capital letter and to end the sentence with a full stop.

On analysis of Gary's line the following next steps in a teaching and learning strategy emerged. Tom decided to continue enabling him to experience aural and oral activities within a phonic programme so that more consonants were represented and mapped out accordingly alongside corresponding

Figure 5.1 'Raindrops on cars'

graphemes. To continue teaching common high frequency words, for example 'to', 'the', 'in', 'of', guided group work focused on sonorous (open) and occlusive (closed) vowels. Gary should continue to initiate ideas through guided reading and writing sessions (socio-cognitive strategy) and continue to develop his understanding of the connections between what is read, spoken, heard and written. The teacher needs to give Gary opportunities to demonstrate his understanding of those whole-language connections.

The second child, Robert, contributed 'drip drip' as his line to the group poem (see Figure 5.2). This is a very interesting illustration in which Robert demonstrates his complete connection and engagement (the domain of 'conation', in Huitt 2003; Allal & Ducrey 2000) with his understanding of the theme of rain. Robert explicitly linked the abstracted mapping of those phonemes ('Dp Dp'); he has followed the three sequences of hearing the word, isolating the letter 'D' and representing the letter grapheme. Robert evidences that he is very aware of the format demands of the genre of poetry writing and demonstrates a very effective use of a short sentence. It is interesting to note that Robert did not write 'The water is dripping'. He uses initial and final phonemes to represent whole words as single units of meaning. He uses a large handwriting style (grapho-motor processing) to write in single letters as Robert is still at the experimental phase. Beginning writers' production is not

Figure 5.2   'Drip drip'

automatised, 'they could constrain the written production in many ways for example, the written texts produced by children are shorter and of lower quality than oral ones, due to the cognitive demands of basic transcription skills' (Silva et al. 2010, p. 50).

To further engage Robert in the writing experience and the ownership of that experience Tom planned to encourage Robert to make more use of the role-play area and the writing centre. In this context Robert would enjoy practising using different scripts and styles. He needs to experiment with a range of different materials in the art area to encourage fine motor skill development and spatial awareness. His growing consonant framework needed development to enable more sounds to be heard and represented by Robert. The teacher is aware of the need to avoid Robert becoming enculturated within the model that in school 'learning to write is reduced to conquering a code, the exercise becomes a surface imitation of genre and text-types without being rooted in what is the core of language' (Nilsson 2010, p. 2). Rather, learning should be founded on and around the needs and interests of children as they naturally develop; in too many cases 'writing is given to them from without' (Vygotsky 1978, p. 117).

Rebecca wrote her line 'Splashing in my puddles' (see Figure 5.3) and her illustration clearly depicts the content of what she views as her central message.

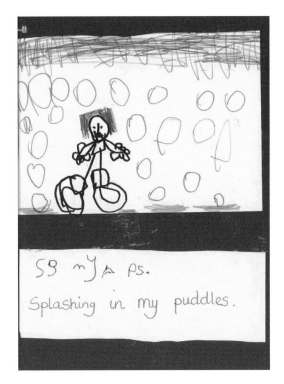

Figure 5.3 'Splashing in my puddles'

Observation of Rebecca's picture reveals a level of maturity and specificity in matching her words to the image, and the identifiable strands of hair on her illustrated figure exemplify this. This illustration demonstrates the importance of talking with a child around a theme and consequently scaffolding the child's developing cognition (Wells 2001a). Rebecca demonstrates the importance to the young writer of conceptualising words as separate units of meaning and represents her words using an initial and final phonemic framework. She is experimenting with lower and upper case formation and some elements of cursive style awareness ('e' 'the'). To support Rebecca's progress as a writer she will work with her teacher on developing an extended phonemic framework and consistent use of lower case letters, both visually, orally and aurally. In her guided group sessions she will continue to develop her understanding of open and closed vowels and CVC words (Consonant Vowel Consonant e.g. 'cow' 'cat' 'dog'). Tom will continue to support Rebecca's enthusiasm and development as a young author through encouraging her to make her own books, either alone, in pairs with the group or with an adult. Topping (2001) suggests that collaborative writing helps participants to structure their thoughts, it can support the higher-order skills of planning, intelligent questioning, reorganisation and restructuring to counter-balance the traditional focus on mechanics and the final product (Boyle & Charles 2011b, p. 10).

Mohamed's line to the poem supplied another interesting illustration which depicts the central message of the raindrops 'plopping' on the street clearly (see Figure 5.4). Note the size of the raindrops which dominate the space on the paper. Mohamed was engrossed in this genuine task because it was self-initiated and this in turn leads to an authentic individual response (Rijlaarsdam et al., 2008). His onomatopoeic choice and use of 'plopping' clearly evokes the sound of the rain as Mohamed conceptualises it. Mohamed is aurally discriminating beyond initial phonemes and is able to represent three or more sounds in a word, for example 'sRNR'. Although he has heard and isolated four sounds in the word 'raindrops', he has confused letter placement by writing the letter 's' at the beginning of the word instead of as the final sound. Mohamed has written two high-frequency words correctly: 'on' and 'the'. For Mohamed's next developmental steps it was suggested he focus on his understanding of final phonemes through aural discrimination. Notice how carefully and with what control Mohammed has coloured in the raindrops. This suggests that he already has good fine motor skills and is developing good hand–eye co-ordination. Therefore, he needs more practice in forming letters through self chosen activities in a writing area context (role play). It was suggested that structured small-group sessions would support this experimental stage of development.

Charlotte initiated an illustration from a known/familiar rhyme that connected to the theme of 'water'. The content of the poem was solely originated by Charlotte and she was enabled to explore her own understanding

Figure 5.4 'Raindrops plopping on the street'

of rhythm and rhyme by connecting with the detailed illustration. Her artwork facilitates her writing process, resulting in a text that is richer in sensory detail and more intricate than the most traditional writing- first crayon-drawing-second approach (Smagorinsky & O'Donnell-Allen 2000). Charlotte has demonstrated a high level of written competence. Her two sentences contain word constructions that signal a growing orthographic knowledge that goes beyond a consonant framework, with an exploration of vowel sounds – albeit sometimes incorrectly used. The reader can notice from Figure 5.5 how Charlotte has started the process of editing and self-correcting her text which demonstrates that she is reading for meaning in a real context (Berninger 2001). Charlotte would benefit from support in developing her knowledge/awareness of initial consonant clusters (for example she uses 'sd' instead of 'sp' for spout) and the correct use of vowels through consonant vowel consonant work (CVC). A logical step would be to extend her use of prepositions and high frequency words and to explore the specific position of digraphs ('sh' for 'washed'). Charlotte should be encouraged to write personal narratives (developing their content) as she has already demonstrated her enthusiasm to sustain text production.

Figure 5.5 'Incy wincy spider'

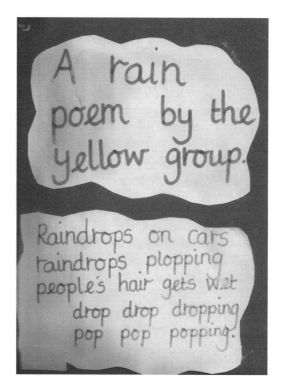

Figure 5.6 'Group poem'

Then the children jointly composed the group poem (see Figures 5.1 to 5.6) by reading and arranging the lines which they had written separately. They liked the sound and order of the lines as the poem came together. They all decided that Charlotte had too many lines and Charlotte was happy to have an individual poem all of her own. 'Accountable talk seriously responds to and further develops what others in the group have said, it puts forth and demands knowledge that is accurate and relevant to the issue under discussion' (Resnick et al. 1998, p. 5).

Conclusion

This article has only the space and scope to represent one small case study of the whole-class work on this theme using its normal guided group pedagogy; that is a clear limitation in scale in substantiating its findings to the reader. However, within those limitations, it is focused on a group of five children developing their writing skills based around the socio-cognitive apprenticeship model of writing (Englert et al. 2006) and an understanding that writing and learning to write are interdependent competencies (Rijlaarsdam et al., 2008). The diverse range expressed in the children's written poems and illustrations exemplifies each individual being enabled to self-regulate their impressions of the weather instead of replaying back to the teacher an imposed model 'from without' (Perrenoud 1998; Vygotsky 1978). While detailing the use of the guided group strategy to support writing development, we also explored a model of group work working with a teacher as collaborator and co-constructor (Allal & Ducrey 2000).

The chapter exemplifies how guided group teaching has the potential to provide a context in which the complexity and abstractions of the writing process can be tackled by young children. It is important that group composition is carefully considered so that children feel that they can collaborate openly in a caring and sharing environment. Writing is a sensitive self-revealing process – whatever the age of the writer – and each child needs to feel affectively secure (Allal & Ducrey 2000) in revealing their feelings and emotions in print. For children to be taken through their zone of proximal (or potential) development (Vygotsky 1978), social interaction has to be supported and managed by the teacher (Smith 1996). We stress that teachers need to develop within group work approaches which enable them to explore and develop pupils' creative thinking and problem-solving strategies. Obviously the zone of proximal development cannot be the same for all children, so teachers' 'adaptations will need to be differentiated to take account of these variations' (Heritage 2011, p. 69). To quote from Perrenoud 'to the extent that pupils do not have the same abilities nor the same needs or the same way of working, an optimal situation for one pupil will not be optimal for another ... one can write a simple equation: diversity in people + appropriate treatment for each = diversity in approach' (Perrenoud

1998, pp. 93–94). Teachers therefore need to be trained and confident in understanding children's trajectories of learning (Heritage 2011), and how they progress through a learning trajectory. This demands that the teacher has assured pedagogical content knowledge (Shulman 1986) with the capacity 'to transform the content knowledge he/she possess into forms that are pedagogically powerful and yet adaptive to the variations in ability and background presented by the students' (Shulman 1987, p. 15). It follows that teachers and their trainers have to re-think the basis of pedagogy: synonymous with this process is an understanding that a pupil as an autonomous learner should be involved in sharing the construction of his/her own learning, that is, self-regulated learning.

CHAPTER 6

AN ANALYSIS OF A GUIDED GROUP'S STORY WRITING

Introduction

This case study describes a strategy which supports the affective domain development of children. This process involves a deepening understanding of balancing transcription processes (motor aspects) with the need to reduce the cognitive demand on working memory for the young writer (modelling/ scribing). We address the problem of young children who find difficulty in developing their writing skills and in some cases do not see themselves as writers in the current climate of coverage, pace and measurable outcomes (Boyle & Charles 2011; Dunsmuir & Blatchford 2004). We describe a strategy which enables children to feel good about engaging in the complex process of writing. It describes how in working with Year 1 children (5–6 years of age) we developed a process to support and report writing development 'within the social mediation of learning' (Allal et al. 2005; O'Brien & Neal 2007). As a result of this pedagogical intervention, we refined a specific process (guided group work) and a structure for analysis to identify each individual writer's range of learning needs. Collaboration in the process enabled us to deepen our understanding of how to identify individual writing needs and to support affectively the development of each emerging writer (Myhill 2006; Perrenoud 1998). A major part of this process involved a deepening understanding of balancing transcription processes with the need to reduce the cognitive demand on working memory for the young writer (Bourke & Adams 2010; Flower & Hayes 1986), in short, a nurturing pedagogy (Goouch 2008).

In addressing the development of early years writing, teachers should be aware of the learning needs of the child as s/he develops as an emerging writer in a highly complex problem-solving activity (Allal et al. 2005; Bereiter

& Scardamalia 1987; Boyle & Charles 2010a; Flower et al. 1986). Our empirical work (Boyle & Charles 2010b, 2011) has deepened our understanding that although the technical (cognitive) development of the child as writer is essential, this development will not take place without an equal support for the child's affective/conative domains (Allal & Lopez 2005; Boyle & Charles 2010a, 2011; Perrenoud 1998; Riggs 2004). Throughout the period of the research, we practised the mutual interdependence of cognition and the affective/conative domains in supporting children's learning: 'Conation can be thought of as "an internal engine" that drives the external tasks and desires. It is the interconnected network of energy that transforms ideas into action. This is the "work domain" which is the connective tissue that puts knowledge (cognitive domain) and feelings (affective domain) into action' (Riggs 2004, p. 3). Case study research (Boyle & Charles 2010a, 2011) has evidenced the motivational effects on young children as writers when they have been enabled to express themselves through being given the freedom to explore their own ideas and interests in composition. Lambirth and Goouch (2006) support this assertion that young writers need freedom 'to express themselves beyond the parameters of the National Literacy Strategy' (p. 146).

The complexity of the transcriptional and translational processes needed to become a writer requires that the child is not taught within a predominantly whole-class structure, with its demands for completion within fast-paced time limits (Alexander 2004; Myhill 2006; Myhill & Locke 2007). The technical demands, for example graphemic realisation of writing (symbols have meaning), alphabetic principles (letters represent speech segments), sound symbol connections (e.g. the letter 'a' can have a different sound based on its position in a word), left to right directionality alongside the process demands (e.g. auditory non-verbal reading comprehension, knowledge of various text structures, mapping letters to words through handwriting), are child specific and demand differentiated teaching (Perrenoud 1991, 1998; Boyle & Charles 2010b). The child should build and hone competency in two broad areas: transcription and translation of ideas. Each of these contains a number of sub-skills: transcriptional aspects involve everything from physically producing texts to spelling correctly and producing accurate grammar; while the translation processes involve generating and organising information (Emig 1971), of which planning and editing are a part (US Department of Education 2008, p. 2). The emerging writer requires sustained recursive individual opportunities to engage with the experiences which take the child through the steps of 'mark making' to the abstractions of written composition. Many teachers struggle to understand how children develop writing skills and its associated complexities 'when writing instruction should begin and how to organise and implement an individualised writing programme?' (Bloodgood 2002, in Martin et al. 2005, p. 236). This complexity is identified by Keen (2010) and Graham,

Harris and Mason (2005), illustrating that development of writing skills depends on changes in children's strategic behaviour, knowledge and motivation. It is now recognised that 'skilled writing for what it is, is a tremendously complex problem-solving act involving memory, planning, text generation and revision' (Bruning & Horn 2000, p. 26). The child cannot change alone, 'if classroom instruction offers superficial [undifferentiated whole class] low level tasks, it is doubtful if children will engage in thoughtful and strategic ways' (Paris & Paris 2001, p. 93).

Equally central to supporting the child through this complexity is 'the guiding nurturing force of the teacher whose conceptions of writing will provide a model for and shape [children's] beliefs. We argue that programmes for developing writing motivation will rest on the beliefs that teachers themselves hold' (Bruning & Horn 2000, p. 26). For children to become strategic and have an understanding of their own learning requirements, optimal conditions require that the children are trained as self-regulated learners (Graham et al. 2005; Perry et al. 2007; Schunk & Zimmerman 1997; Zimmerman 2008). Vygotskyian philosophy is at the heart of these interactions as in its operation learners actively construct knowledge: 'This recognises the importance of the interactions of … teacher–student discourse in the classroom' (Vygotsky 1962, in Arapaki & Zafrana 2004, p. 45). However, children do not independently arrive at this position and this demands that teachers change from a didactic to a more child-centred pedagogy that leads to the recognition of a child's zone of proximal development (Vygotsky 1962, 1978). Perry et al. (2007) "observed writing activities in five Grade 2 and 3 classrooms and characterised them as 'high' or 'low' in opportunities for children to engage with self-regulated learning (SRL): In 'high' SRL classrooms, pupils engaged in complex, meaningful writing activities, [they] made choices and had opportunities to control challenge in completing tasks. They received support from their teachers and peers which was 'instrumental to their Self-Regulated Learning' (Perry et al. 2007, p. 30). Where this support from teachers is lacking, pupils will find it difficult to make the step. Unfortunately, these pedagogical confusions are common. For example, our research survey data have evidenced that:

> despite the very high percentage of teachers reporting their prioritisation of formative assessment, schools clearly have very different definitions of what it is and what is its purpose. The understanding of formative assessment (or its synonym Assessment for Learning [AfL]) and its practical operation is poor so there is no clarity of definition. (Boyle & Charles 2010b, p. 298)

Therefore, the teachers are not in a skilled professional position to provide the specific individualised support required to scaffold pupil learning and development (Sadler 1989).

Methodology

It is a first principle that if you are teaching children as a whole-class group, rather than planning your teaching and learning around individual learning needs, then you cannot be teaching formatively. If you teach without differentiation then how can you be matching learning to each child's developmental needs (Boyle & Charles 2008, p. 22). This philosophy was nested in the Better Schools report (DES 1985) and its four founding principles – to be broad, balanced, relevant and differentiated. We feel that using the guided group strategy in a differentiated classroom balances learning needs common to all students with more specific needs tagged to individual learners (Tomlinson 2001, p. 4). For McAdamis (2001), 'differentiation allows the teacher to focus on the same key principles for all students, however, the instructional process, pace and rate towards understanding these concepts varies' (p. 3).

The Williams report states that: 'guided group work offers an organisational approach where attention can be given to particular children who may require additional support or challenge to ensure that they continue to progress in learning' (Williams 2008, p. 67). Here, a health warning is needed: the guided group should not be misconstrued (from Williams's definition) as a group needing special needs support; the opposite is in fact the case – a guided group is the optimal teaching, learning and assessment situation in which the lead professional in the classroom is focused on individual learning support. The Department for Children, Schools and Families (DCSF 2007a) also recognised the importance of these 'organisational changes' as a move away from the dominance of whole-class teaching. However, our definition and use of guided group pedagogy is more systemic and yet formative than the DCSF's. A guided group teaching and assessment session involves the teacher working with a group of no more than five children; less than five is equally valid when appropriate but the group size must enable children to collaborate and to contribute orally. More than five children in the guided group makes it difficult for the teacher to carry out analytical observations and interrogations, which are essential for formative analysis to take place to support learning. The guided group is focused on 'the importance of inquiry, construction and collaboration rather than the delivery of outcomes' (Wells 2001a, p. 2). The teacher is trying to identify learning strengths and misconceptions, and to do that s/he has to facilitate opportunities for all the children in the guided group to demonstrate their learning in an open, equitable and trusting context. The teacher will be focusing either on re-visiting, consolidating or introducing a new teaching point and will be assessing how the children assimilate the learning. Following an opening whole-class presentation and the allocation of challenging writing tasks across the groups of children in the class, s/he is primarily focused on the guided group s/he is working with. This will maximise the interaction and dialogue with those five children for the duration of the 20–25-minute session.

In the guided group context, integration of the cognitive, affective and cona-tive domains is optimised (Allal & Ducrey 2000) for the child to be authentically involved in his/her own learning. In the guided group there are only a small number of pupils being taught together so the teacher is not easily distracted from his/her focus on teaching and learning; the child feels able to contribute more readily because of the group size, the proximity of the teacher and the collaborative learning ethos being engendered. The teacher needs to be aware that children do not make learning progress without that affective domain (moti-vation, enthusiasm, self-esteem, interest, sense of well-being) being integrated with the cognitive and conative (putting the interest of the affective domain into practice, the praxis) (Allal & Ducrey 2000; Huitt 2003; Riggs 2004). A guided group session offers the optimum opportunity for those effects to be maximised to the benefit of the learning progress of all the children in the group.

The evidence presented in this chapter shows the work of four children in a guided group and their progress across two sessions in narrative genre writ-ing supported by teacher analysis.

We determined upon a teaching strategy to support the children through story writing by using a guided group methodology and adopting a develop-mental framework based on Applebee (1978) and Depree and Iversen (1994). Depree and Iverson's framework is based on planning a programme that caters for children's individual cognitive, conative and affective needs and that provides opportunities for group learning activities (p. 11). Applebee's framework is based on analysing six stages in children's event-arrangement of stories (heaps, sequences, primitive narratives, unfocused chains, focused chains and narratives) in young children (1978, p. 72). In addition, Hudson and Shapiro's (1991) partial framework for studying narrative production was also incorporated with specific reference to the development of four types of knowledge and skill: (a) content knowledge; (b) structural knowledge; (c) micro-linguistic knowledge; and (d) contextual knowledge (p. 89). Finally, we agreed on the minimally accepted characteristics of the structure for a single episode story: (a) a formal beginning (e.g. once upon a time) and ori-entation to introduce setting and characters; (b) initiating events-goal directed actions; (c) a problem or obstacle to achieving the intended goal; (d) a resolution of the problem; and (e) a formal ending device (Hudson & Shapiro 1991, p. 100). These frameworks enabled us to observe, record and act upon the chil-dren's writing development: 'A method of observation and interpretation that could wholly reveal them' (Voss 1983, p. 5). We agree with Allal and Lopez (2005) in seeing teaching, learning and assessment as part of a 'triadic system linking the teacher, the learner and the knowledge being dealt with' (Allal et al. 2005, p. 250). Similarly, Perrenoud's research highlights the importance of 'differentiated teaching which attempts to place each pupil in a situation which is optimal for him to the extent that pupils do not have the same abilities, nor the same needs, nor the same way of working; an optimal situation for one pupil will not be optimal for another' (Perrenoud 1998, p. 94).

The work of four children is used to exemplify our approach and the type of analysis undertaken to support the young writers. To enable our analysis we used an instructional framework of questions (Depree & Iverson 1994) such as: Did the child enjoy listening to a range of stories read by the teacher? How did the child demonstrate this engagement? While observing the child writing his/her assessment, did he/she appear to be enjoying the task? What are the child's psycho-motor skills? Do these include levels of co-ordination, dexterity, strength, speed, fine and gross motor skills? Were the children at the single phoneme, consonant framework, multiple phonemes, whole word construction stage? Were the children able to retain, internalise and transfer the whole or parts of a story? (Boyle & Charles 2011).

Data and discussion

The class had been working on 'traditional stories' as part of a five-week theme. 'Goldilocks' was one of the traditional stories which the children had experienced as part of their Literacy programme. The first piece which the guided group wrote is based on that story. Their second piece of writing, written five weeks later, was a story about an imaginary journey which was stimulated by classroom work on the topic of 'journeys'.

Child One: Xenab at the start demonstrated a lack of confidence (see Figure 6.1) and did not appear to view herself as capable of producing written text like her peers. 'Difficulties in schooling can be explained in the differences between pupils, often described as failings or shortcomings in pupils who do not reach the norm: socio-cultural handicap, linguistic poverty, poor family background and lack of motivation and support; so many expressions which stigmatise pupils in difficulty' (Perrenoud 1998, p. 93). It was apparent that Xenab's affective domain (intrinsic motivation, self-esteem) needed support, and from the provision of that support it was hoped that her confidence in herself as a writer would develop. Teaching strategies utilised to address this included involving Xenab in the (metacognitive) process of analysing her own writing with support. We ensured that she had consistency of conditions within the guided group with whom she talked and wrote collaboratively during teaching sessions. Young learners learn to write from correctly contextualised modelling (Berninger et al. 2006) and within this collaborative process, miscues were discussed and resolved (Boyle & Charles 2011).

Child Two: Hana's reluctance to orally retell her version of the story to the rest of the group was indicative of her overall shyness. However, through the means of a guided group strategy she listened to the other children retell their stories which provided her with prompts and important sequential events. Hana required oral support with repetition of each phrase/sentence she chose to write. She was able to use her growing sight vocabulary to read and then write the beginning of her story from the prompt 'bubble' ('one' 'day' 'went'

Found task V. difficult → could not retell story (orally). Some confidence locating words — eg 'Goldilocks' 'bears' → could not transfer this in all of the sentence. Could not re-read what she had written (Took 20 mins to do above).
Develop stories → orally/aurally → shared writing.

Goyilocks went
to the bears
he's shexpet
the bates rep

Figure 6.1   Xenab's story of Goldilocks

'bears'). Hana's story (Figure 6.2) using Applebee's (1978) construct of story suggests that it has elements of a 'focused and unfocused chain'.

> When a child is able to create a story with a main character at the centre who then goes through events that are linked … based on Vygotsky's concept theory (1962) the organisation is not conceptual but a pseudo concept … before true concepts emerge children make use of pseudo-concepts which are superficially similar but which remain perceptually rather than conceptually based. (Applebee 1978, p. 62)

Hana understands the structure of a story but has not learned to focus and give the story direction; there is some cohesion to the events of her story and little content as it abruptly trails off in its conclusion (Simmons & Gebhardt 2009).

Research on the merits of guided group teaching and learning (Hayes 2008; Tomlinson 2001) and on how the value of reading aloud to children affects vocabulary development (Robbins & Ehri 1994; Whitehurst et al. 1999), acquisition of literary syntax and vocabulary (Purcell-Gates et al. 1995), and story text (Duke & Kays 1998). However, researchers have found a negative relationship between the amount of time teachers spend on reading aloud in Kindergarten and children's decoding skills (Meyer et al. 1994). These studies suggest that merely reading books aloud is not sufficient for accelerating children's oral vocabulary development and listening comprehension. Instead, the way books are shared with children matters (McGee & Schickedanz 2007, p. 742).

Child Three: Burhan retold his version of the story to the group and his enthusiasm and enjoyment spilled over into his narrative characterisations (voice, actions, phrases) in which the teaching roles became de-regulated (Perrenoud, 1998) and the guided group in Vygotskyan (1978) terms 'had a greater opportunity to understand, internalise and therefore lay down the foundations for the development of dialogical skills that support text production' (Rijlaarsdam et al. 2008, p. 60). Burhan did not require any oral support for his written account of his story or any additional support for his spellings. Using Applebee's (1978) construct of story, Burhan's written piece (Figure 6.3) suggests elements of a 'focused chain' alongside some aspects of 'narrative'.

> Narratives expand on the focused chain by including additional features. The centre of the story is developed while a new idea or circumstance develops out of a previous idea. This propels the story forward, often ending with a climax, in narrative everything is held together by the core which relies on abstract or concrete bonds. (Simmons & Gebhardt 2009, p. 3)

And in a 'true narrative', the incidents are linked both by centring and chaining and are more fully controlled (Applebee 1978, p. 69). Burhan

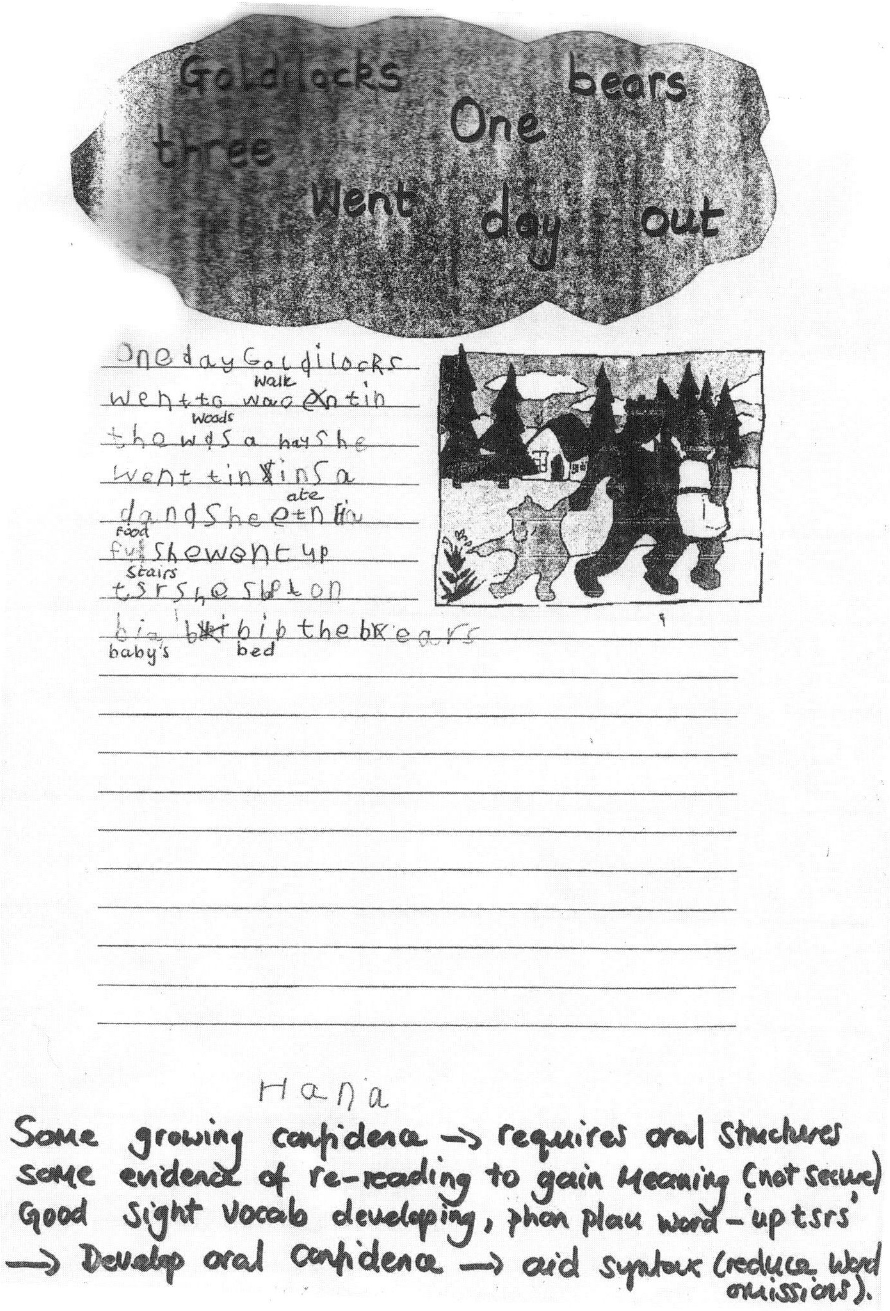

Goldilocks   bears

One

three

Went   day   out

One day Goldilocks
went to woods xnt in
                  walk
            woods
the wds a hay she
went tin tin sa
dand she etn tin
                ate
ful she went up
food
t s r s e slet on
stairs
big bibib the brears
baby's   bed

Hana

Some growing confidence → requires oral structures
some evidence of re-reading to gain meaning (not secure)
Good sight vocab developing, phon plau word – 'up tsrs'
→ Develop oral confidence → aid syntax (reduce word
                                            omissions).

Figure 6.2   Hana's story of Goldilocks

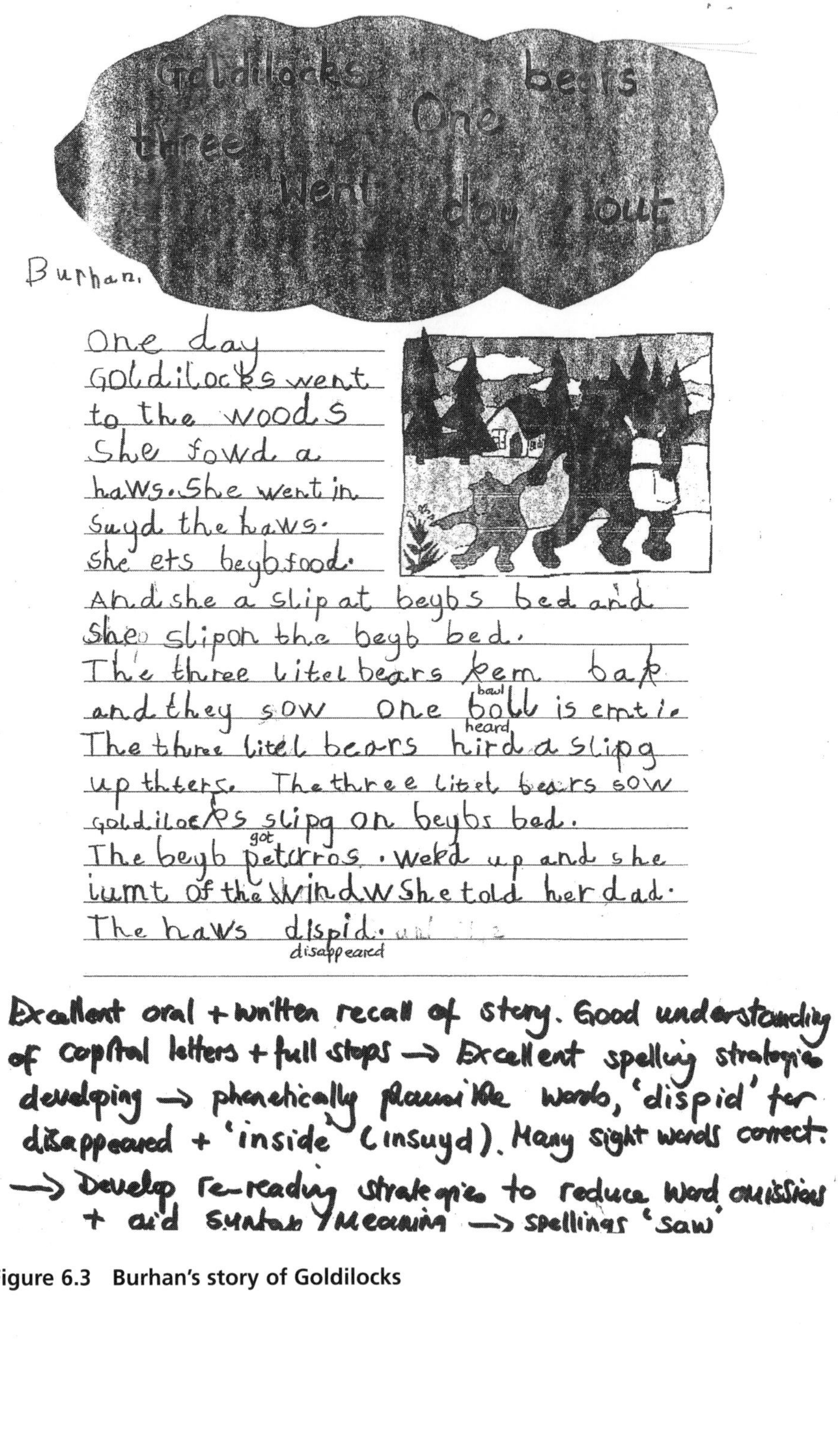

Goldilocks beais three One Went day out

Burhan.

One day
Goldilocks went
to the woods
she fowd a
haws. She went in
suyd the haws.
she ets beyb food.
And she a slip at beybs bed and
She slip on the beyb bed.
The three litel bears kem bak
and they sow one boll [bawl] is emtie
The three litel bears hird [heard] a slipg
up thters. The three litel bears sow
goldiloeks slipg on beybs bed.
The beyb peturros [got] · wekd up and she
iumt of the windw she told her dad.
The haws dispid. [disappeared]

Excellent oral + written recall of story. Good understanding
of capital letters + full stops → Excellent spelling strategies
developing → phonetically plausible words, 'dispid' for
disappeared + 'inside' (insuyd). Many sight words correct.
→ Develop re-reading strategies to reduce word omissions
+ aid syntax / meaning → spellings 'saw'

Figure 6.3   Burhan's story of Goldilocks

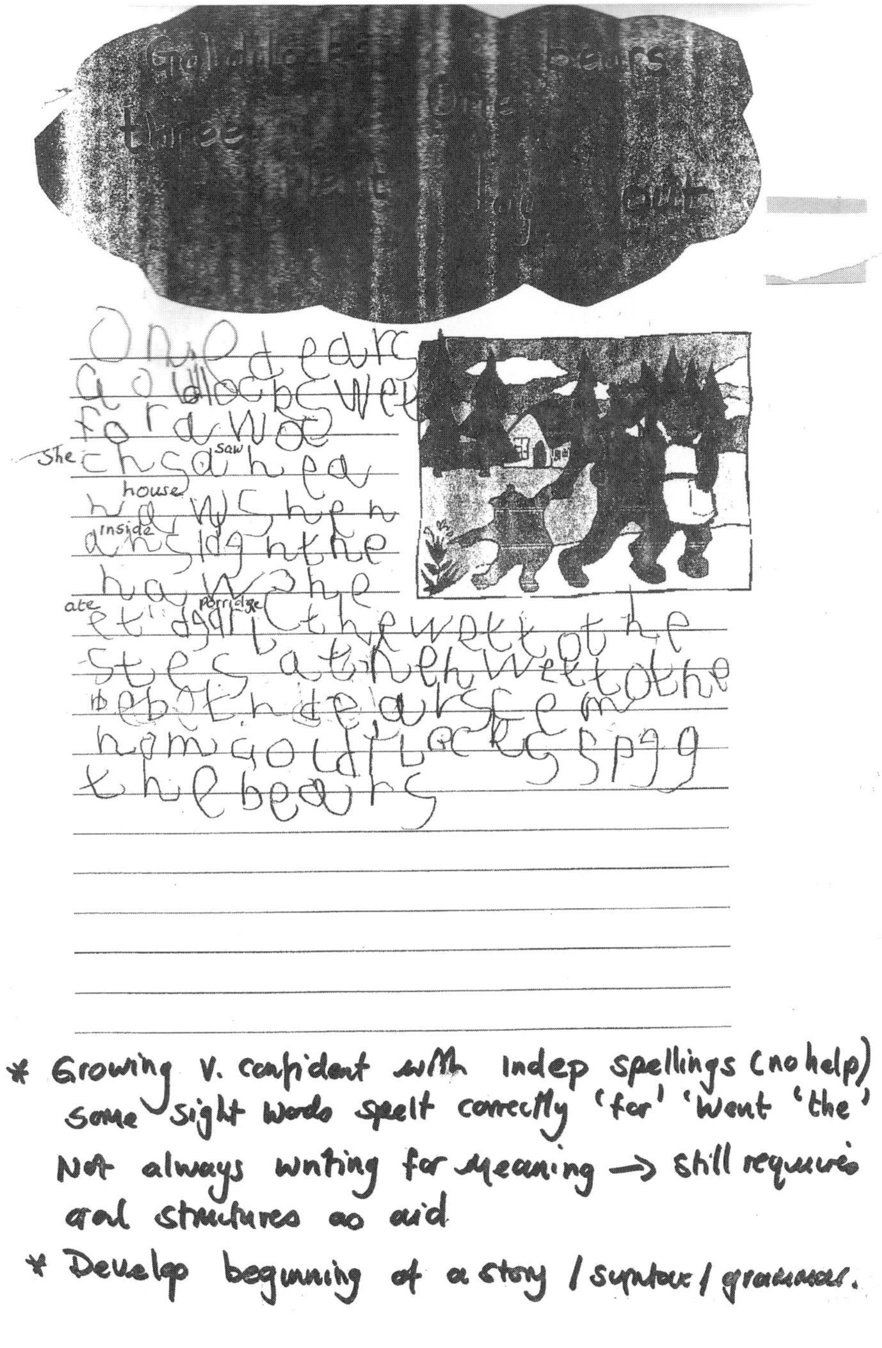

(child's handwritten story with teacher annotations: "She", "saw", "house", "inside", "ate", "porridge")

The child's writing reads approximately:

One bears
a blocbe well
for a wos
chsa hea
hny when
lg n the
ha whe
eti ther wett of he
stes a then well to the
the bears mothe
nom Goldilocks spgg
the bears

Teacher's handwritten notes:

* Growing v. confident with indep spellings (no help)
  some sight words spelt correctly 'for' 'went' 'the'
  Not always writing for meaning → still requires
  oral structures as aid
* Develop beginning of a story / syntax / grammar.

Figure 6.4   Sultan's story of Goldilocks

understands the structure of a story but is limited in syntactical, grammatical and text cohesion features which result in a loss of flow to his story. However, his creative imagination and awareness of audience is developing, note how he concludes his story: 'The house disappeared'. The importance of Burhan's ending is significant in this context, as he is the only member of the group to write one. In an attempt to understand Hana and Xenab's omission of a story ending, Berninger et al. (2006) draws attention to an understanding that 'language is not a unitary construct ... and that Language by Ear, Language by Mouth, Language by Eye and Language by Hand, are each complex functional systems that draw on common as well as unique processes to achieve different goals' (p. 62). This suggests that Hana and Xenab were constrained by transcription processes and the demand on working memory to complete conclusions to their stories (Bourke & Adams 2010; Flower & Hayes 1986).

Child Four: Sultan's oral retelling of the story featured elements that he found interesting and important as events in the story. His written account (Figure 6.4) demonstrates that he does not always write for meaning as he confuses the word 'bear' for 'day' in his opening sentence. He writes predominately in the correct tense and occasionally confuses his use of prepositions. Stein and Albro (1997, in Sénéchal et al. 2008, p. 30) suggest that children who produce well-structured stories must organise the events that occurred in a sequential meaningful way. Sultan's story, with its predominant constraints on Language by Hand (Berninger et al. 2006) is clearly following a sequential series of events through 'focused and unfocused chains' (Applebee 1978).

The second piece of narrative writing continued within the guided group format. Because we felt that Applebee's framework was limiting their analysis in this instance we decided to use Hudson and Shapiro's (1991) narrative framework. We felt that the latter was more structurally comprehensive and provided more elements to the stories which enabled richer analysis. The children were asked to write an imaginary journey stemming from the original Big Book entitled: 'Biff's aeroplane'. The children collectively composed their version of Biff's journey:

> One cold day Biff wanted to take her aeroplane to the park. Biff wished that her aeroplane was magic so she pretended if she pulled the string it would go to new places. Biff got smaller and the aeroplane got bigger. She got inside and went to London to play in the zoo with the animals. Biff got tired and got bigger and went home.

As the teacher scribed the children's ideas, they were encouraged to keep re-reading the text to maintain cohesion and the overall flow of the story. Burhan chose to narrate his idea of 'pulling the string to get smaller to fit into the plane' and Xenab (Figure 6.5) decided to include 'London' as a location when asked by the teacher, 'where will Biff travel to when she is in the plane?'. The question 'What will she do when she is there?' enabled Sultan to respond: 'Play in the zoo with all of the animals'. Hana chose not to orally contribute in the group's composing process. Burhan concluded the story with 'Biff got tired and got bigger and went home'. Fisher and Williams (2000) remind us that story writing for children 'provides them with the most complex of intellectual challenges' (p. 70). All the richness of the dialogue used by the group hasn't been captured in the brief version of the story above.

Guided group story writing is one of the processes in the social construction of learning. Vygotsky (1978) stated that '[children's] learning is socially constructed during interaction with others and the relationship between literacy and social interaction is complex and significant to their learning' (p. 243). Although the stories generated by the four children share similar content knowledge, closer analysis reveals differences in structural, micro-linguistic and contextual knowledge (Hudson & Shapiro 1991, p. 89). Three of the stories contain a formal beginning – 'One day' (Xenab), 'One snowy day' (Burhan), 'One sunny day' (Hana) – while Sultan has no formal beginning. Interestingly, Xenab's opening is the only story to attempt 'an orientation to introduce setting and characters' (Hudson & Shapiro 1991, p. 100): 'Biff was playing in the park'. The other three stories introduce a character with no setting: 'Biff pulled the string of the aeroplane' (Sultan), 'Biff has an aeroplane' (Burhan), 'Biff pulled the string of the aeroplane' (Hana). (Figure 6.6). All four of the stories assume audience awareness and do not give any background information as to the central character's actions, motivations and intentions. Hindi and Hildyard (1983, in Hudson & Shapiro 1991) and Kemper (1984, in Hudson & Shapiro 1991) suggest that the 'inclusion of internal goals, motivations and reactions making more sophisticated story productions are absent from children's fictional stories before the age of around 8 years' (in Hudson & Shapiro 1991, p. 101).

'In initiating events-goal directed actions' (Hudson & Shapiro 1991), three of the stories include references to this aspect of narrative construction, as Burhan, Sultan and Hana wrote: 'Biff pulled the string of the aeroplane'. Xenab omits this structural element and wrote: 'Biff went to London'. Interestingly, all four of the children locate the central character in place and/or time (Sultan uses no time reference). The inclusion of cumulative events to add coherence feature in Hana and Sultan's stories: 'It flew higher and higher. Biff got smaller and smaller' (Hana); 'It went faster and faster Biff got smaller and smaller' (Sultan). In contrast, Burhan (Figure 6.7) uses the theme of 'shrinking' (which he initiated during the group composition) to conclude his story and moves away from a traditional/conventional ending. Xenab does not include any reference to 'shrinking' which may suggest, as Hudson and Shapiro (1991) propose: 'For young children, the fit between the structure of knowledge and memory and the structure of the narrative genre is critical in determining narrative coherence … and the amount of translation involved between knowing and telling' (p. 126).

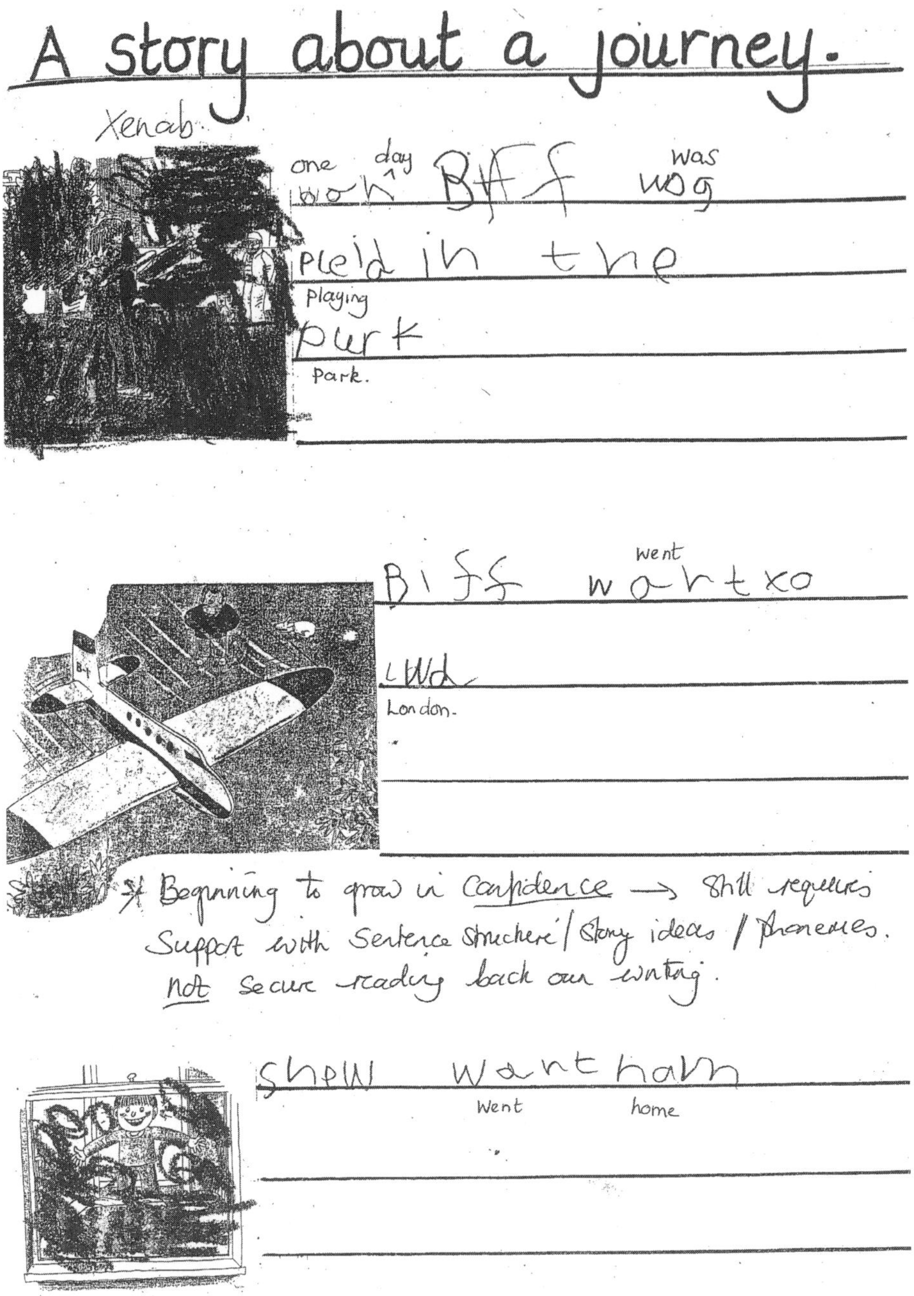

A story about a journey.

Xenab

one day BIFF was
woh playing in the
park purk

BIFF went wortxo
LWd
London.

※ Beginning to grow in Confidence → Still requires
Support with Sentence structure / Story ideas / Phonemes.
Not secure reading back our writing.

shpW wantham
Went home

Figure 6.5 Xenab's story of an imaginary journey

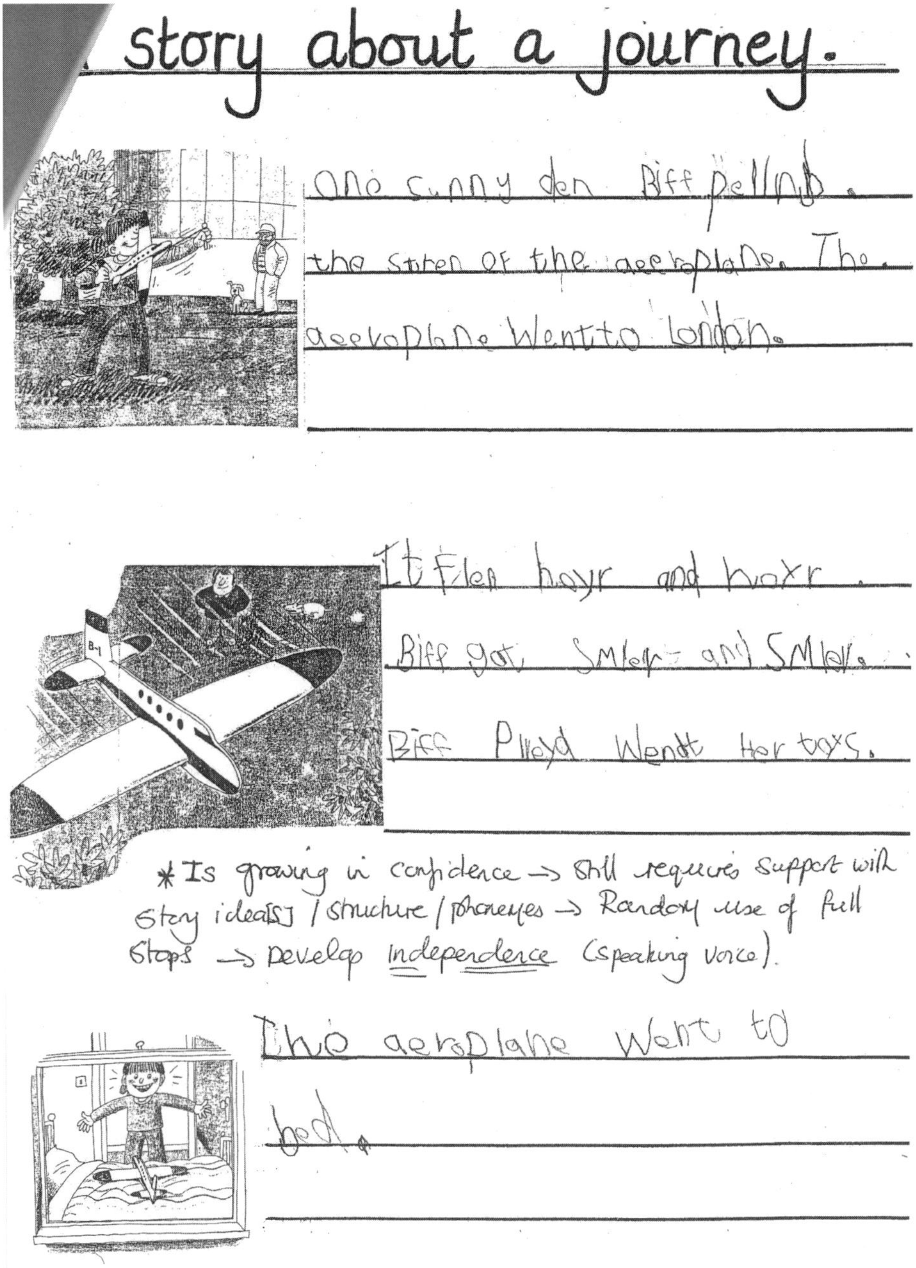

story about a journey.

One sunny den Biff pelind
the striren of the aeroplane. The
aeroplane wentito london.

It Flen hayr and hayr.
Biff got smler and smler.
Biff Pllayd Wentt Her toys.

*Is growing in confidence → still requires support with
story ideas / structure / phonemes → Random use of full
stops → Develop independence (speaking voice).

The aeroplane Went to
bed.

Figure 6.6   Hana's story of an imaginary journey

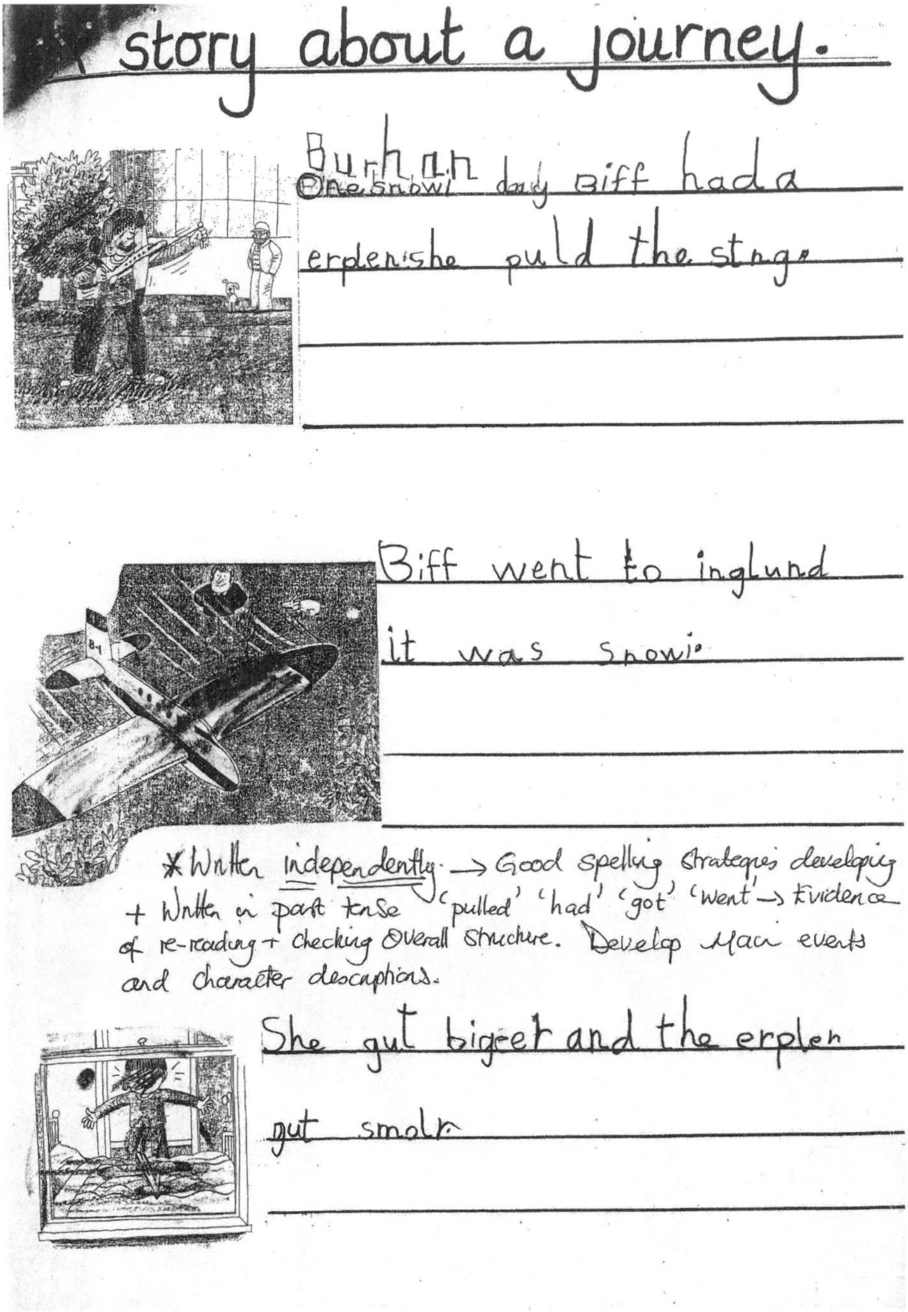

story about a journey.

Burhan

One snowl day Biff had a erplen she puld the stinge

Biff went to inglund it was snowi.

*Written independently. → Good spelling strategies developing
+ Written in past tense 'pulled' 'had' 'got' 'went' → Evidence
of re-reading + checking overall structure. Develop Main events
and character descriptions.

She gut bigger and the erplen gut smolr.

Figure 6.7   Burhan's story of an imaginary journey

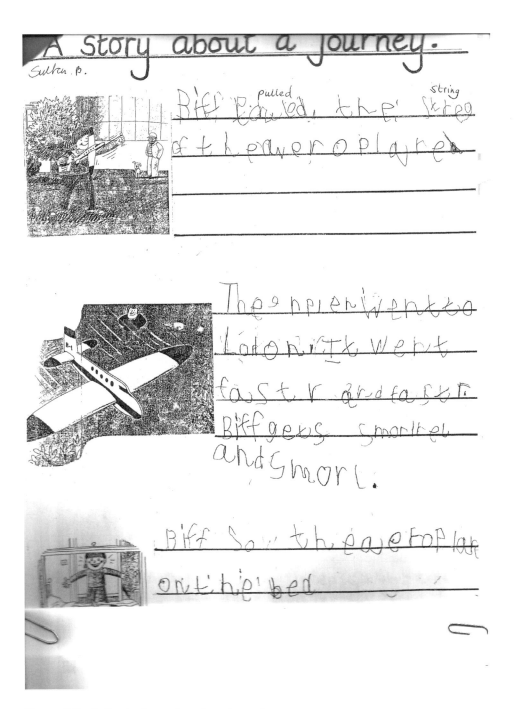

Figure 6.8   Sultan's story of an imaginary journey

All four children give minimal narrative detail in their stories and the structural coherence specifically with regard to representing 'a problem or obstacle to achieving the intended goal and a resolution of the problem' is absent in their writing (Hudson and Shapiro 1991, p. 100). Their central character, Biff, travels on a journey (achieving the intended goal) in all of the stories. However, Sultan and Hana begin to develop how this goal was achieved: 'The aeroplane went to London. It went faster and faster. Biff gets smaller and smaller' (Sultan); 'It flew higher and higher. Biff got smaller and smaller' (Hana). In contrast, Xenab provides no detail of how this goal was achieved: 'Biff went to London'; similarly Burhan: 'Biff went to England. It was snowy'. There are varying degrees of implied reader awareness across the four stories that generate quite different questions for different children: 'Why did Biff get smaller' (Sultan and Hana); 'How did Biff get to London?' (Burhan and Xenab). Is this more about memory, cognitive load, physical constraints on transcription, narrative awareness, motivation or lexical limitations in any analytical attempt to explain the differences across the four stories?

The fusion of illustrations and the children's writing is seen as a 'visual literacy integral to the composing process' (Boyle & Charles 2011, p. 12). Curtis and Bailey (2001) agree that 'pictures provide something to talk about … and can be used to reinforce literal, critical and creative thinking' (p. 11). All four of the children appear to conclude their stories. Burhan's ending 'she got bigger and the aeroplane got smaller' suggests a movement into another episode in which the reader is left with an air of expectancy and mystery. Similarly, Sultan's ending: 'Biff saw an aeroplane on the bed' (Figure 6.8) suggests that he has not given his narrative a 'formal ending device' (Hudson & Shapiro 1991, p. 100). In contrast, Hana and Xenab's endings are more definitive in their description: 'she went home' (Xenab); 'the aeroplane went to bed' (Hana). Pradl (1979) observes that children reach the end of their 'inventiveness span' fairly quickly and will abruptly finish stories with tag endings' (p. 23). Each of the children provides a different ending to the same illustration. Smith (1975, in Protheroe 2010, p. 33) suggests that 'many children find pictures difficult to interpret' and Pressley (1977, in Protheroe 2010, p. 33) argues that 'children need training before they can interpret representations of three-dimensional space in two dimensions'.

A more conceptual analysis as proposed by Protheroe (2010) who suggests that understanding is not simply a matter of taking a literal interpretation of the meanings in a text … 'meaning requires an interaction of information from the text with background knowledge … and the inferences that they make' (p. 36). In short, all four of the children do not go beyond the illustrations except when each narrative reaches a 'high point' when travelling to London. For the writer, the developmental necessity of 'knowledge-based inferences can provide missing information, resolve discrepancies and predict unmentioned facts or events' (Mason & Just 2011, p. 314).

Conclusion

The study involved a relatively small number of teaching sessions and only reports on the first two stories, so cannot and does not claim to be conclusive. However, it does demonstrate that on a small scale, close analysis guided by acknowledged research frameworks can be effective in supporting teaching pedagogy (Salvetti 2001, p. 79).

We addressed the issue of 'one size fits all' in teaching writing to emerging writers through utilising sound research methodologies in the field and a classroom structure of a guided group to address the children's affective, conative and cognitive domains simultaneously. Applebee's (1978) framework enabled us to analyse the young writers' stories against a conceptual structure. His six stages provided an initial understanding of how story developed for the children, from a simple 'heaping' of events through to well structured narratives. The second analytical tool used was that of Hudson and Shapiro (1991), based on the characteristics of the structure for a single episode story: (a) a formal beginning; (b) initiating events; (c) a problem or obstacle to achieving the intended goal; (d) a resolution of the problem; and (e) a formal ending device (p. 100). In addition, Hudson and Shapiro's (1991) partial framework for studying narrative production was also incorporated with specific reference to the development of four types of knowledge and skill: (a) content knowledge; (b) structural knowledge; (c) micro-linguistic knowledge; and (d) contextual knowledge (p. 89).

Through using these analytical frameworks specific information about each child's progress was obtained and we were able to scaffold support based on those individual learning needs. Because of this information and the affective domain environment of the guided group, we suggest that improvement in the children's stories was facilitated between story 1 and story 2 through this nurturing pedagogy (Goouch 2008). For example, Xenab still required support with scribing to lessen her cognitive load and enable her to focus on her other needs, narrative structure, spelling and cohesion while she develops as an independent writer. This collaborative process within the guided group can be described as the establishment of 'a socio-cognitive apprenticeship in which teachers and students collaborate, inform, question, think aloud, self-correct, challenge and construct meaning together' (Englert et al. 2006, p. 211).

In short, this should become a core pedagogical strategy for Xenab to develop as a story writer. Similarly, Sultan still requires strategies to support cohesion and narrative development, but his dominant need is motor development and transcription, mapping by hand (Berninger 2006). In contrast, Burhan is already demonstrating that he has been exposed to a wide range of narratives and his need is for knowledge-based and evaluative-based inferences (Mason & Just 2011). He does not necessarily need illustrations to structure his storytelling. Finally, Hana requires a paired collaborative approach (Charles & Boyle 2011; Topping 2001) to facilitate the oral aspect of story rehearsal, reducing the pressure on her for a written output.

CHAPTER 7

INTRODUCING EARLY YEARS CHILDREN TO THE IMPORTANCE OF NON-FICTION FOR THEIR WRITING DEVELOPMENT

Introduction

The focus of this chapter is on non-fiction as a macro-genre and the development within early years children's non-fiction writing of expository (informational) texts.

The chapter's case study focuses on a group of five-year-olds working initially from a story/narrative of the *Owl Babies* (Waddell & Benson, 1992) extending from that interest in to non-fiction and the development of a reference book about owls. The children's illustrations initiate their subsequent text and form the basis of their ideas, which are facilitated and scaffolded by the teacher acting as scribe. Although the three processes (listening to the story; visualising their illustration; composing their text) were common across the group, the time-on-task varied from one session completion to three days completion, with time, space and pace allowed accordingly.

The concept of genre refers to:

> abstract, socially recognised ways of using language. It is based on the idea that members of a community usually have little difficulty in recognising similarities in the texts they use frequently and are able to draw on their repeated experiences with such texts to read, understand, and perhaps write them relatively easily. (Hyland 2007, p. 149)

	A procedure	**A report**
Purpose	Tells how to do something	Informs reader about something
Structure	Goal – materials required, steps needed	Identifying statement
Grammar	Imperatives, action verbs, describing words Adverbials to express details of time, place, manner Connectives, sequences	General nouns, relating verbs Action verbs, timeless, present tense Topic sentences to organise bundles of information

Figure 7.1   Features for procedures and reports

Source: Hyland (2007, p. 153)

Most learners will, at a basic level, be able to recognise that there are six basic factual genres within the overall concept of non-fiction: recount, report, discussion, persuasion, explanation and instructions. Research evidences that primary school age pupils get a great deal of experience of writing recounts but rarely experience the other genres (Wray & Lewis 2000, p. 112). Therefore, the learners need to be exposed to and supported in their understanding that a macro-genre, like a newspaper, might be composed of several sub-genres, such as exposition, discussion and a rebuttal. Figure 7.1 shows that even very young learners can understand the social purposes of these genres, the ways they are staged and their significant language features.

Within this framework it is important that young writers learn that non-fiction authors write for specific purposes. They write to describe, to persuade, to explain, to entertain, to tell a personal story and to provide instructions. Writers at all levels need to realise that non-fiction writing is a rich tapestry of text-types that differ dramatically in form, structure and features. Writers need to be able to explain that a note, a poem, a laboratory report, a history paper, a literary analysis and a persuasive poster all have unique purposes, differing degrees of formal language and specific physical attributes (Stead & Hoyt 2012, p. 7).

Genre pedagogies

Genre-based pedagogies through writing instruction offers pupils an explicit understanding of how target texts are structured and why they are written in the ways that they are. This explicitness gives teachers and learners something to aim for, making writing outcomes clear rather than relying on hit and miss inductive methods, whereby learners are expected to acquire the genres they need from repeated writing experiences or the teachers' notes in the margins of their work. Providing writers with the knowledge of appropriate language forms shifts writing instruction from the implicit and exploratory to a conscious manipulation of language and choice (Hyland 2007). Consequently, learners are in the process of being empowered to become autonomous and self-regulated. In addressing the development of early years non-fiction writing, the practitioner should be aware of the learning needs of the learner as the learner develops as an emergent writer in a highly complex problem-solving activity (Flower et al. 1986; Scardamalia & Bereiter 1986). The complexity of the structural and developmental processes needed to become a non-fiction writer requires that the learner is not taught within a predominantly whole-class structure, with its demands for completion within fast pace time limits. The emerging writer requires sustained recursive opportunities to engage with the experiences which take the learner from the steps of mark-making to the abstractions of written composition. This complexity is identified by Graham, Harris and Mason (2005) in that its development depends on changes in a learner's strategic behaviour, knowledge and motivation (p. 207). Allied to this it is now recognised that 'skilled writing for what it is, is a tremendously complex problem-solving act involving memory, planning, text generation and revision' (Bruning & Horn 2000, p. 26). The learner cannot change alone: 'if classroom instruction offers superficial [whole-class] low level tasks it is doubtful if learners will engage in thoughtful and strategic ways' (Paris & Paris 2001, p. 93). However, 'many teachers struggle to understand how children develop writing skills, when writing instruction should begin and how to organise and implement an individualised writing programme' (Bloodgood 2002, in Martin et al. (2005) p. 236). Equally essential to this complexity is 'the central guiding nurturing force of the teacher whose conceptions of writing will provide a model for and shape [learners' beliefs]. We argue programmes for developing writing motivation will rest on the beliefs that teachers themselves hold' (Bruning and Horn 2000, p. 26). For learners to become strategic and to have an understanding and awareness of their own learning requirements, optimal conditions require that the learners are trained as self-regulated learners (Graham & Harris 2000; Graham et al. 2005; Perry et al. 2007; Schunk & Zimmerman, 1997, 2007). This Vygotskyian philosophy is at the heart of these interactions as learners actively construct knowledge. This recognises the importance of the interactions of teacher–student discourse in the classroom (Vygotsky 1962). However, learners do not independently arrive at this position and teachers need to change from a didactic to a more learner-centred pedagogy that leads to the recognition of a child's zone of proximal development.

A central tenet of our formative philosophy is the location of the child at the centre of learning (Freire 1970; Goouch 2008; Perrenoud 1998; Vygotsky 1978):

> when learning floats on a sea of talk, intermediate age learners develop skills in collaboration, inquiry, partnership and deep thinking. They learn to take a position and explain it to others. They learn to share a point of view and develop a strong sense of audience. With collaboration and shared conversation, non-fiction writing takes on its own strength and purpose. (Stead & Hoyt 2012, p. 7)

However, the majority of literature in this area shows that the child is deprived of agency and locates the child as a passive recipient (Hartman 2002), with material delivered and information supplied by the teacher 'from without' (Vygotsky 1978). Consequently, there is a prevalence of teacher-centred lessons on elements of compartmentalised non-fiction which are irrelevant for some children in a class and not matched to the interest levels of the individual. This chapter explores, through a case-study approach, a group of five-year-olds working initially from the story of 'The Owl Babies', then extending from that into interest in non-fiction and the development of a reference book on owls.

In our research attempting to locate and quantify the extent to which the genre of non-fiction is being utilised in early years writing programmes, a profile of limited access to and use of such texts emerged. One study of 20 Year 1 classrooms (children aged 5–6) found that informational texts consti-tuted less than 10 per cent of classroom libraries. We discovered that over 90 per cent of the books in the classrooms surveyed were fiction and the non-fiction books were primarily for reference: textbooks, encyclopaedia, diction-aries and the like. Outside of school about 80 per cent of the reading adults do is non-fiction, for example newspapers, magazines, memos, manuals (Zinsser 1989, in Harvey 2002). Another study recorded that an average of less than 3 per cent of the materials displayed on classroom walls related to informational texts (Duke 2000) – display materials at this age largely sprang from story or recount writing. 'The six main types of non-fiction genre they identified were recount, report, procedure, explanation, argument, discussion and of these recount was overwhelmingly the most widely experienced by children in school' (Wray & Lewis 1996, p. 9). Duke's research evidenced that pupils in Year 1 classrooms spent an average of only 3.5 minutes each day interacting with informational texts – even less in low socio-economic status schools (2000, p. 41). In 2006 the Revised Literacy Framework was introduced in England, in which genre types were allocated specific time slots through-out the year.

We feel that it is not enough to simply provide access to books and mate-rials. We need to:

- Read non-fiction aloud
- Explore non-fiction to satisfy curiosity
- Use non-fiction for instruction
- Read non-fiction to do research
- Read non-fiction to write it well
- Skim non-fiction to answer questions
- Show the particular features of non-fiction – the titles, headings, bold print, graphs, charts – and point out the purpose of these text elements (Maxim 1998, in Harvey 2002, p. 16).

To develop these ideas further:

Read non-fiction aloud: Reading non-fiction aloud will help the development of a sharper, more discriminating aural capability for the learner. This will be achieved through presenting technical/sophisticated forms of language within contextualised frameworks, for example 'owls are carnivorous and possess eye-cones'. Traits such as spelling and sentence structure will develop hand-in-hand within the context of instructionally rich writing opportunities; for example, the development of an understanding of adverbs and how to use them. Adverbs are especially useful because they help non-fiction writers to describe actions, for example with adverbs we can write about moving slowly, cautiously, quickly, painfully or tiredly. For instance, a sentence could read: 'Quietly the snake slithers towards the sleeping frog' (as opposed to 'the snake slithers towards …') (Stead & Hoyt 2012, p. 14).

Explore non-fiction to satisfy curiosity: The real world is rich, satisfying and compelling to young minds. As Einstein said, 'I have no real talents, I am only passionately curious'. This passionate curiosity is shared by young learners. It is natural and does not need to be forced within artificial teaching situations, rather it needs recognition then 'feeding', nurturing, supporting and scaffolding in contexts of real, shared, interactive, collaborative investigations.

Use non-fiction for instruction: For example, a piece of instructional writing conveys the importance of structure, chronology, sequence and a specific use of language imperatives and specific language demands. However, it is important to be aware that chronology as a sub-skill can require flexibility, for example, asking children to write about the order in which the ingredients of a cup of coffee are used in its making can differ through custom and experience. There will still be an acceptable end product, a cup of coffee, however, strict adherence to the same chronology of use of ingredients may not be the case across a sample of children. Conversely, in the process of 'getting dressed' strict adherence to the order of 'under' and 'outer' garments is required.

Read non-fiction to do research: In the context of our emerging writers, 'research' is defined as adopting, cultivating and developing an awareness of perspective, critique and bias. These factors will take on different forms depending on the entity or context being researched, for example natural phenomena, people, places, etc. Stead and Hoyte (2012) give an example in terms of developing perspective on a topic relevant to the children – the time allocated to lunch break. What is their perspective? Do they appreciate the length of time (one hour in the playground)? What do they think the teachers do in the lunch break? Is there enough time for the teachers to do what they do? In Figure 7.2 the results of another group of young children's poll data on animals and their habitats are shown (Figure 7.2). Herein demonstrates the multiplicity of research activity by the children – they are not regurgitating facts but are being required to take a position and form a view.

Hamsris are verry cyoot.
mis ett chees.
fish swim about.
bugees fli a lot.
rabits hope a bout alot.

Hamsters are Very Cute.
Mice eat Cheese.
Fish swim about.
Budgies fly a lot.
Rabbits hop about a lot.

Figure 7.2   'All animals are in cages'

Writings about Christopher Columbus have become classic examples of misinformation spread as truth. For centuries children have grown up celebrating Christopher Columbus as the discoverer of America – even though we know that he did not discover America. The continent was already richly inhabited by people with sophisticated cultures and with a possibly more liveable lifestyle than that of Europe at the time (Mann 2002).

> With a stance towards critical literacy we can guide students to read about Christopher Columbus and about the Vikings who explored the area two hundred years earlier and then read about the highly developed cultures and agricultural talents of the native North American tribes. With this broad base of perspectives, non-fiction writers can engage in thoughtful conversations that go far beyond a simple recounting of dates and events. (Stead & Hoyte 2012, p. 19)

Read non-fiction to write it well: Expecting young learners to write non-fiction well demands that the teacher and practitioner provide explicit modelling within real and authentic structuring. Alongside official curriculum requirements, opportunities that emerge from the pupils themselves provide enormous space for them to explore, research and write about their chosen theme/subject. For example, in an early years classroom we noted how the children became absorbed as each day several woodlice appeared in the space in which they played on the carpet. The children made some very interesting initial observations: 'They always come out from under the radiator', 'Are they insects?', 'Why are some of them white and brown?', 'Why are they inside our classroom?' This prompted the children to do their own research about woodlice and make their own colourful posters and books (Figure 7.3a-d) displaying important information for the rest of the class to share. Some of their statements included: 'Woodlice like to live outside in damp areas', 'Woodlice are not insects but are crustaceans', 'They will die if they cannot get to water'. This theme also provided a further contextualised context for the rest of the class to explore other related crustaceans, their habitats and feeding preferences.

Skim and scan non-fiction to answer questions: Skimming and scanning are two very different strategies for speed reading. Skimming refers to looking only for general or main ideas and works best with non-fiction (or factual) material. With skimming it may be assumed that this is a haphazard process pacing the eyes wherever they fall. However, to skim effectively there has to be structure but without the need to read everything. For example, doing research on a long chapter or a website, by reading the first few paragraphs in detail will give a good idea of what information will be discussed. Once the direction of where the reading is headed is established, the reading of only the first sentence of each paragraph can begin. At the end of each topic sentence, your eyes should drop down through the rest of the paragraph, looking for important pieces of information such as dates, names or events. Unlike skimming, when scanning, you look only for a

Figure 7.3a–d   Reception class children's woodlice books

specific fact or piece of information without reading everything. For scanning to be successful, pupils need to understand how material is structured as well as comprehend what is read, so they can locate the specific information they are looking for. Scanning also allows the reader to find details and other information in a hurry. The material you scan is typically arranged in the following ways: alphabetically, chronologically, non-alphabetically by category, or textually (Beale 2013).

Non-fiction to enhance pupils' understanding

Howard Gardner's seminal text, *The Unschooled Mind: How Children Think and How Schools Should Teach*, stresses the importance of teaching for understanding. In it he critiques modern-day educational schooling systems as 'paying lip-service to goals like "understanding" or "deep knowledge" [as] they, in fact, prove inimical to the pursuit of these goals' (Gardner 1991, p. 5). Gardner's criticism strongly suggests a conflict between the unique qualities of each learner and an awareness of 'not fully appreciating just how difficult it is for schools to succeed in their chosen, or appointed tasks … and [not being] cognisant of the ways in which basic inclinations of human learning turn out to be mismatched to the agenda of the modern secular school' (1991, p. 6). Is Gardner implicitly suggesting that a degree of sympathy be extended towards our teachers, senior professionals and support staff trained to teach our pupils? Furthermore, should there be, within this degree of sympathy, some recognition of the macro complexity of the task itself in educating all learners? It is without any contention that one of our fundamental principles is that teaching is an incredibly complex and demanding vocation. However, it appears that Gardner is explicitly criticising the failure of the schooling system to teach for understanding based on the individual and the relevance of the knowledge/information/curriculum to those individual needs.

> Even when school appears to be successful even when it elicits the performance for which it has apparently been designed, it typically fails to achieve its most important purpose; which is to establish in every student some 'genuine understanding' of what the curriculum offers in its various domains. We have failed to appreciate that in nearly every student there is a five year old 'unschooled' mind struggling to get out and express itself. And that this remains the case after all the scholastic endeavour is done. (Gardner 1991, p. 2)

Harvey (2002) cites an example in which Gardner's daughter, an A student in physics with exemplary grades and very high percentile test scores, telephoned him shaken at discovering that she did not understand physics. 'What do you mean you don't understand physics? You have always been a superior physics student', Gardner responded. She explained that although she had little trouble with the maths and could complete the assignments error free, she did not 'understand' physics. She discovered her lack of understanding when her teacher had flipped a coin and asked the class to explain in writing the physics involved in coin tossing. She could not do it, and it was apparent that years of high marks and stratospheric SAT scores did not guarantee understanding (Harvey 2002, p. 13). A salient reminder perhaps of how teachers are 'teaching to the test' and moving at pace without any conceptual understanding of the recursive, iterative processes of learning situated within a differentiated model of instruction. Perrone (1994) reminds us that 'our students need to be able to use knowledge, not just to know about things; understanding is about making connections among and between things, about deep and not surface knowledge and about greater complexity, not simplicity' (Perrone 1994, p. 3). Non-fiction enhances our understanding, it allows us to investigate the real world and inspires us to dig deeper to inquire and better understand (Harvey 2002).

Modelling desirable 'genre' behaviours

We hear many teachers and practitioners asking: 'How do I get my pupils to write better quality non-fiction pieces?' and we initially respond with 'modelling'. 'But isn't that simply copying from the teacher?' is usually one of the misconceptions that we address and discuss. Modelling desirable behaviours such as technical vocabulary, syntax, sophisticated phrasing, interest levels (enjoyment), text features, and so on, create not only contextualised learning spaces but situate the learning to enable the gradual hand-over or 'uptake' of the concepts being grasped. Also synonymous with modelling is scaffolding, Feez (1998) describes this methodological model as 'the teaching-learning cycle'. Here, the teacher provides initial explicit knowledge and guided practice, moves to sharing responsibility for developing texts, and gradually withdraws support until the learner can work alone. The key stages of the cycle are:

Setting the context – revealing genre purpose and the settings in which it is commonly used;

Modelling – analysing representative samples of the genre to identify its stages and key features and the variations which are possible;

Joint construction – guided, teacher supported practice in the genre through the tasks which focus on particular stages or functions of the text;

Independent construction – independent writing by students monitored by the teacher; and

Comparing – relating what has been learnt to other genres and contexts in order to understand how genres are designed to achieve particular social purposes. (Feez 1998, p. 28)

This iterative process enables pupils to enter the cycle at any stage of their development and understanding of the genres being studied. It does not, however, advocate a 'one-size-fits-all' pedagogy, rather the model clearly supports a differentiated needs-specific approach, in which there are provided 'repeated opportunities to engage in activities which require [the children] to reflect on and critique their learning by developing understandings of texts, acting on these through writing or speaking, reviewing their performance, and using feedback to improve their work' (Hyland 2007, p. 160). Practitioners can also adopt specific 'cognitive openers' in their teaching groups which are a signal to the learner to cue in for specificity, for example as the teacher says: 'Watch how I …', 'Notice the way I …' or 'I am about to show you …'. The pupils are focused in such a way that it is almost impossible during whole-class teaching but achievable during small guided group teaching. 'Through close observation writers are more likely to notice the techniques that empower non-fiction writing, tune in closely during a think-aloud, and hold their breath in awe as they watch how onomatopoeia and creative punctuation bring voice and life to a piece of writing' (Hoyt 2011, p. 5).

However, this learner-centred model has the potential to be misunderstood and misapplied in the classroom. It is not about teacher control and the domination of teacher voice; on the contrary, it requires movement towards deregulation of teacher and teacher roles in order that the learners' capacity through their voice, participation and genuine contribution be allowed to flourish. Indeed, Hoyt (2011) perceptively observes that 'meta-linguistic awareness' will help writers to understand that they are not gathered around the chart to be entertained (or controlled), they are there to learn how to engage in a particular writing behaviour (p. 5). Creating, planning and supporting these desirable behaviours through careful modelling and scaffolding does not happen overnight, nor must it be assumed that it will happen successfully for every learner. Genre pedagogies are not without their implications. Frater (2004) argues that the explicit teaching of literary technique may result in formulaic writing, so that individuality and creativity are stifled and pupils lack any sense of ownership (p. 80). Graham (1998) shared this concern and describes 'teachers using counter-productive mechanical tasks' (p. 117), while Gibbons (2001) argues against 'grafting techniques on to non-willing children' (p. 16). However, it seems that supporting young writers is a very skilful business that requires knowledgeable, sensitive teachers; scaffolding must be gradually withdrawn so that pupils can become independent creative authors. Teachers need to assume a variety of teaching roles beyond that of 'expert' and respond contingently to the needs of their learners as they discuss, plan, draft and re-draft their written work. Pupils can benefit from experiencing what it is like to be an 'author wrestling with problems, drawing on knowledge and experiences, seeking advice and responding to critical moments' (Corden 2007, p. 10). The criticisms laid out above do have some credence to them, however Hoyt (2011) cogently reminds us that:

> during read-alouds, we read as an adult, delivering the reading selection with fluency, expression and dynamic interpretation; we do not read-aloud like a young child, so the same high standard for performance and delivery should be evident when we write in front of pupils. Modelling writing is a time to pull out all the stops and to generate non-fiction text that elevates expectations and paves the way for excellence. (p. 4)

Similarly the theoretical underpinning of psychologists such as Vygotsky (1978) and Bruner (1990) gives recognition to the importance of collaboration and scaffolding. Together these concepts assist learners through two notions of learning: 'shared consciousness – the idea that learners working together learn more effectively than individuals working separately. Borrowed consciousness, the idea that learners working with knowledgeable others develop greater understanding of tasks and ideas' (Hyland 2007, p. 158). The degree of teacher intervention and the selection of tasks therefore play a key role in 'scaffolding writing, representing a cline of support from closely controlled activities to autonomous extended communication, reducing direct instruction as the learner gradually assimilates the task demands and procedures for constructing the genre effectively' (Hyland 2007, p. 158).

What we did

We worked with Fatima, an early years trained teacher only in her second year of teaching but already demonstrating vestiges of a child-centred pedagogy; she was teaching in a medium sized faith primary school. The school population totalled 653 pupils and was organised as four form entry, age stratified.

Children were actively involved with the teacher in their learning and were working on an owl project. The project had been kick-started by a visit to the class by an owl-keeper who brought in a selection of owl breeds for a class assembly. Following this there was much lively discussion and the teacher read owl stories and showed their illustrations. The children were very enthusiastic to write and draw their own owl pages, featuring habitats, feathers, food and babies. Working in collaboration they produced their own illustrations and then wrote their sentences. It is worth reinforcing that collaboration does not mean that they copied from each other's ideas in their guided group situation or in any way sacrificed individuality.

The children's work

Charlotte's main emphasis in her illustration is to convey her understanding of the texture of her owl's feathers (see Figure 7.4). She had very carefully

Figure 7.4   Charlotte's owls have rough and smooth feathers

selected materials which enhance her tactile and sensory exploration of the subject and match her description of the owl's feathers. This extended process encouraged her to widen her vocabulary with an increased and interesting use of the adjectives 'rough' and 'smooth'. She could have written a less effective sentence: 'They have feathers'. Charlotte is working in a semi-phonetic phase and sometimes uses two, three or four letters to represent a whole word. She has 'the ability to notice, mentally grab hold of and manipulate these smallest chunks of speech' (Yopp & Yopp 2000, p. 130). Charlotte uses a consistent sound-symbol correspondence and demonstrates a growing sight vocabulary, for example 'the[y]', 'and'. Her emerging understanding of the complex and necessary interplay between the visual, oral and aural aspects is demonstrated through the digraph 'th' as she consistently uses it in its medial and final position in two separate words ('smooth', 'feathers').

From Fatima's analysis of Charlotte's description of her owl, the following next steps in teaching emerged. Charlotte needs support and scaffolding by Fatima to develop her knowledge of the phoneme 'y' and of medial vowel placement. Charlotte needs encouragement to practise her handwriting through self-chosen activities in the role-play area and the writing centre, for example through shopping lists and invitations to parties, etc., appointments for the doctor and designing cards for different occasions.

Tom illustrated two mature representations of owls whose colour and shape have been clearly well thought through and detailed (Figure 7.5). It is interesting to note how he has attempted to show movement in his drawing as one owl appears to be in flight and the other is stationary. This demonstrates how important it is that children are allowed and enabled to be in control and to make autonomous editorial decisions about every aspect of their work. Tom is writing within a semi-phonetic phase and is reliant on the sound structures of words demonstrated by his use of two or three letters to represent whole words. Tom has a growing awareness of standard spelling ('the', 'and') and is developing his understanding and use of capital letters and full stops. On analysis of Tom's writing, Fatima decided that she needed to work with Tom to support him in his development of phonemic awareness through initial consonant clusters and vowel phonemes. She needs to continue supporting the link that Tom has begun to establish between reading and writing to build his genre-specific vocabulary. Fatima will model short, imaginative and factual texts, explaining to the young writers their purpose and intended audience, Corden (2007).

Ryan chose to illustrate a scene in which, in his words, 'The owl flies very silently'. In listening to and reading the information that Fatima presented about owls and their lives, he has captured the image of the owl flying silently as his chosen focus. Ryan's illustration shows this purpose as he attempts to portray one owl flying among the trees (Figure 7.6). Notice how he has selected six different colours to represent his owl. This suggests that he was motivated and interested and wanted to take his time in completing his representation. Ryan is working at a semi-phonetic phase, relying heavily on the sound structures of words. He uses two, three and four letters to represent whole words, however, he qualifies the verb with two adverbs. Ryan reads using one-to-one correspondence of written text and recognises that print conveys a constant message (Fatima observed that he returned to read

Figure 7.5   Tom's illustration and description of two owls

the same text successfully at different times). On her analysis of Ryan's piece, Fatima decided to increase his phonemic knowledge through working on the visual and aural aspects of word construction, also specifically the 'y' phoneme and medial vowel representation. Fatima also wanted to introduce

Figure 7.6   Ryan's owl is flying very silently

Ryan to working with lines on his paper to aid orientation of letters and words and 'sweep return' motion.

Jamie chose to illustrate owls at night. His illustration is interesting on two levels: firstly, he has selected material to portray the concept of night very carefully (black paper, silver stars) and secondly, he has drawn two mice in the distance (Figure 7.7). He orally described why the mice were there, 'because the owls look for food'. This demonstrates that Jamie was not yet conceptually ready to write this additional sentence but he was enabled, through his illustration, to talk about and extend his intention.

Jamie is aurally discriminating within an initial and final consonant framework. His attempt at writing the word 'at' which shows a definite space between each of the two letters suggests he is not yet secure with some words as cohesive units of meaning. Note how Jamie has attempted to organise the directionality of his sentence through a demarcating line. Fatima's analysis caused her to identify the following teaching steps with Jamie. She wanted to increase his phonemic knowledge awareness of consonant clusters and their compositional function as letters in words. Fatima was also conscious that Jamie needs opportunities to work through his use of a space to denote a new word within a sentence and identify its meaning.

Kate's illustration has been carefully conceptualised and designed using mixed media to depict the owl chick's feathers using small vertically shaped straws (Figure 7.8). Kate is working predominately at an initial phonemic stage and represents each word with a single phoneme (with the exception of 'bs' for beaks). She has a growing awareness aurally and graphemically of vowel discrimination. Note how Kate omits the words 'egg', 'with' and 'their' from her sentence. She makes an attempt to write 'with' but flips 'w' over into an 'm'. From observation and analysis of Kate's drawing and writing, Fatima decided she needed to secure Kate's knowledge of the alphabet: she would subsequently work on this through a range of aural, oral and visual activities. In her sessions with Kate (and with Kate's peers with similar needs) she would model sentences of varying lengths from a range of sources and con-texts, for example shared book experiences with her friends.

Hannah's drawing shows the owls chasing mice for their food (Figure 7.9). She has retained this specific information about owls' feeding habits from the reference material presented by Fatima and discussed in the group. Hannah artistically represented her picture in mixed media (lace, crepe paper, and felt tip pens) showing a swooping owl, two mice and the sun. Note also how Hannah has attempted to write her name predominantly using capital letters and a single lower case 'a' (reversed). She is working within a partial alpha-betic phase (Ehri 1992, 1995). This suggests that Hannah was able to identify initial and final phonemes in spoken words, although while making an informed approximation she makes a natural aural confusion between the 'c' and 's' phoneme. Hannah worked exclusively with dominant sounds in a single word (ms = mice), making no attempt at the other words (they, eat). This suggests her lack of connection to the aural, oral and visual cueing sys-tems (Stuart et al. 2008).

Fatima determined from Hannah's work on owls that (Wray & Lewis 1996) 'teacher modelling, joint construction pattern of teaching is vital, for it not

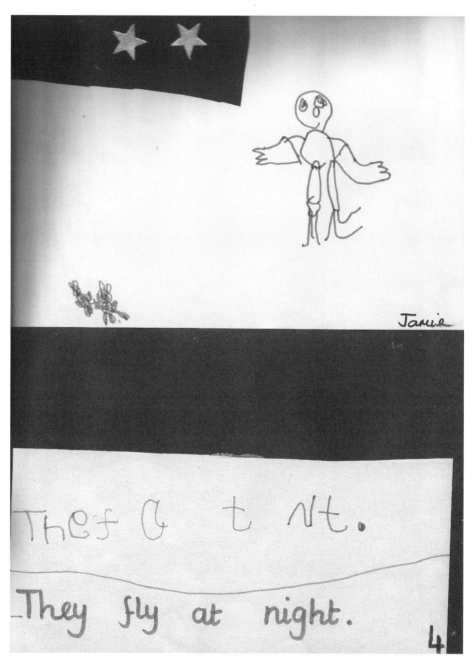

Figure 7.7   Jamie's owl flies at night

only models the generic form and teaches the words that signal connections and transitions but it also provides opportunities for developing children's oral language and their thinking' (Wray & Lewis 1996, pp. 10–11). Fatima

Figure 7.8 Kate's owl babies get out of eggs

therefore will work with Hannah on many oral sessions and sessions in which she (Fatima) acts as a scribe before Hannah is ready to attempt her own framed writing. Hannah requires continued exposure to text construction

Figure 7.9   Hannah's owls eat mice

in meaningful contexts, that is, modelling brief sentences initiated by the child to focus on enlarging her phonemic repertoire. She needs to continue learning correct letters and their placement while writing her name. Hannah does demonstrate through her illustration that she is capable visually but needs scaffolding to reach her potential in manipulating text.

Conclusion

It is important to conclude that these strategies and support mechanisms are not viewed as short-term gimmicks, but are part of an iterative process in which teachers' need to utilise judiously throughout a child's schooling as an essential component of whole school policy.

CHAPTER 8

THE INTEGRATION OF GENRES (NARRATIVE TO NON-FICTION) WITHIN A FORMATIVE PEDAGOGY

Introduction

Our experiences of observing teaching and learning in schools (Boyle & Charles 2010a) have led us to become concerned at the dominant paradigm of a 'pedagogy of poverty' (Hodges 2001) at the expense of a 'pedagogy of plenty' (Banks 1994; Haberman 1991). Bernstein's theory of power and control of education knowledge (Bernstein 1970) is overtly practised in classrooms globally (Alexander 2005, 2008; Boyle & Charles 2010a). This is evidenced in the narrowing of the curriculum in response to the No Child Left Behind initiative in the USA and the centrally imposed National Strategies and Standards agenda in the UK (Boyle & Bragg 2006, 2008). Bernstein's theory is still a means of clarifying the relationships between social class, family income and the education process. It introduced the concept of 'restricted and elaborated codes' (Bernstein 1962a, 1962b, 1973), which has been labelled by its critics as a deficit model for the working-class population (Danzig 1995; Francis 2011). It is our contention that expectations for this new meritocracy have failed to materialise (Powell 2001), and the expectations for equity have been reduced by the prevailing metric. This 'pedagogy of poverty' is now practised in the current 'one-size-fits-all' model of teaching and learning (Alexander 2005, 2008; Myhill 2006; Wyse 2007), operating within narrow accountability and a definition of 'standards' based on a 'testocracy' (Guinier & Torres 2003). This case study demonstrates one teacher using guided group work as a potential strategy for a 'pedagogy of plenty' (Haberman 1991).

Our classroom research (Boyle & Charles 2010a) has left us with an unanswered (as yet) question: Why is it that only a small percentage of teachers have a strong and balanced pedagogical base for their practice? Is it that there is a misunderstanding of the definition of pedagogy? According to Alexander:

> pedagogy is the observable act of teaching together with its attendant discourse of educational theories, values, evidence and justifications. It is what one needs to know, and the skills one needs to command, in order to make and justify the many different kinds of decisions of which teaching is constituted. (2008, p. 29)

This 'pedagogy of plenty' as outlined by Alexander is based on a differentiated treatment of children (Perrenoud 1998) operationalised in the classroom through the strategy of guided group work. This teaching philosophy is based on an understanding that learning flourishes through co-construction and self-regulation (Schunk & Zimmerman 1997, 2007) and the teaching environment requires a balance of affective, cognitive and conative domains (Allal & Ducrey 2000) for every child to have access to the elaborated code (Bernstein 1962a, 1962b, 1973). In short, the child is at the centre of the teaching and learning process and it is the child's needs which should dictate the teacher's planning for learning, not the reverse (Boyle & Charles 2010b). Myhill (2006) suggests that the dominant pedagogical model throughout the period has been and still is that of substantial whole-class teaching which causes 'an orientation towards coverage and elicitation of facts rather than the creation and co-construction of interconnected learning' (p. 34). The profile that has emerged from our research (Boyle & Charles 2010a) is one of teachers reliant on prescriptive, centrally disseminated materials from which 'politicians and bureaucrats are demanding greater conformity of education offerings which are transparent and superficially testable' (Patrick et al. 2003, p. 239). Powell supports this view, stating that 'Selection devices like SAT scores may have given a previously under-advantaged group an admissions advantage but that advantage cannot fairly be characterised as helping to equalise educational opportunity. Opportunity for all was therefore not really broadened' (Powell 2001, p. 73). Bernstein consistently rejected the interpretation of his work examining the relationships between social class, family and the reproduction of meaning systems as stating that working-class language and culture were deficient (Danzig 1995), but maintained that they 'are functionally related to the social division of labour, where context dependent language is necessary in the context of production' (Bernstein 1996, p. 147). For Bernstein the fact that 'schools require an elaborated code for success means that working class children are disadvantaged by the dominant code of schooling, not that their language is deficient. "Difference became deficit in the context of macropower relations"' (Powell 2001, p. 73). There is a continuing danger, in Bernstein's terms, of 'privileging texts', and also the possibility of the 'cultural transmission of contemporary, dominant social principles, through invisible pedagogies' (Goouch 2008, p. 99). The Bullock Report (1975) stated that 'a child is at a disadvantage in lacking the means to explain, describe, inquire, hypothesize, analyse, compare and deduce if language is seldom or never used for these purposes in his (sic) home' (5.8, p. 54). This reinforces the crucial role of the teacher in supporting and structuring children's language development equitably. Tizard et al. (1983) did find in their research that 'the most frequently mentioned aim of nursery education listed by teachers was 'enriching language'. However, the researchers went on to state that 'there was also a significant social class difference in the teachers' talk, with more complex uses being addressed to middle class children than to working class children' (p. 537). A clear definition of 'invisible pedagogy' is given by Hartley (1993) in his attempt to understand connections between constructs of childhood, society and pedagogy. He defines 'invisible pedagogy' as the way in which 'control will be achieved implicitly: that is, the child may re-arrange and personalise the context which has been predefined by the teachers; the child will have the apparent discretion as to what, when, with whom and how he acts within the pre-set arrangement' (Hartley 1993, p. 26).

In England the machinery of the metric starts at three years of age (Early Years Foundation Stage with its 147 assessment scales for 3–5-year-olds, DCSF 2007, introducing the young child to a school culture which is dominated by the 'pedagogy of poverty' (e.g. assessment through testing, asking 'right answer' only questions, 'patrolling teacher', etc.) (Boyle & Charles 2008; Hodges 2001) within the paradigm of the testocracy (Guinier & Torres 2003). Through his consideration of the workings of the types of educational practice, Bernstein 'contributed to a greater understanding of how schools reproduce what they are ideologically committed to eradicating: social-class advantages in schooling and society' (Bernstein 1996, p. 29). In the testocracy, the metric is laid down and teaching and learning becomes a process conforming to the testing metric. Its limitations and the humanistic and social implications are not even considered as flaws in the system: 'test scores correlate with parental income (and even grandparents' socio-economic status) rather than actual student performance' (Guinier & Torres 2003, p. 68). The fact that the testocracy reduces merit and a meritocracy to a meaningless pre-destined ordination is ignored. 'Test-centred techniques are used to ration access to elite higher education as appropriate measures of merit' (Guinier & Torres 2003, p. 69) and 'at no point was any attempt made to reconcile this with an elitist rationing process' (Guinier & Torres 2003, p. 69). The testocracy knows no boundaries but income; it even, as Guinier and Torres found in their research in the USA, redefines merit: 'it moved from an assumption that tests are meritocratic for everyone except people of colour to a larger critique of the way in which the conventional testocracy denies opportunity to many deserving white applicants as well. It changed the definition of merit' (Guinier & Torres 2003, p. 72).

The testocracy is an inevitable part of the 'banking' model of education: 'Four times four is sixteen; the capital of France is Paris'. 'The student records, memorises and repeats these phrases … the teacher turns the students into containers to be filled. Education becomes an act of depositing in which the students are the depositories and the teacher is the depositor, which the students patiently receive, memorise and repeats' (Freire 1970, p. 139). This situation recalls the development of a technical skill such as piano playing: 'the pupil develops finger dexterity and learns to strike the keys while reading music, but he is in no way involved in the essence of the music itself'. Instead of being founded on and around the needs and interests of children as they naturally develop and on their activity, '[education] is given to them from without, from the teacher's hands' (Vygotsky 1978, in Nilsson 2010, p. 2). Galton in his follow-up research to the ORACLE studies in the late 1970s (Galton et al. 1980) found that teacher-centred rather than child-centred pedagogy had increased in the period between 1976 and 1996 (Galton et al. 1999b, p. 33). If teachers are, according to Eraut (1994, p. 243), no longer 'autonomous self-directed individuals' this indicates movement from relative autonomy to the status of a technician.

The basis for the escalation in government interventions (Boyle & Charles 2009) – which began in the mid-1980s with the introduction of a prescribed national curriculum which was 'broad and balanced' (1988 Education Reform Act), national testing (1991), and regular inspection of schools (1994), and resulted in the Standards agenda (DfEE 1997) – was a growing understanding by politicians of the importance of being seen to be intervening successfully in education as a message to the electorate. Through this process teachers were reduced in their autonomy and were being pushed towards performativity (Patrick et al. 2003), becoming more compliant in utilising centrally developed 'one-size-fits-all' materials which in the main focused on the production of test performances at the expense of learning and child-centred pedagogy (Alexander 2005, 2008; Brehony 2005; Patrick et al. 2003; Wyse et al. 2007). The Office for Standards in Education (Ofsted) oversaw the arrangements for raising standards, and it did so with the focus on explicit, direct, whole-class teaching. 'The grip which Ofsted exerted on the teachers and the teacher educators was formal and bureaucratic' (Hartley 2002, p. 90). For the New Labour government post-1997 'the raising of standards has become something of a clarion call. League tables abound. Performance – and its measurement – has become the watchword. There has been a pedagogical drift back to basics, back to whole class, direct teaching' (Hartley 2002, p. 90). The National Literacy (1998) and National Numeracy (1999) Strategies were formally introduced and strongly influenced pedagogy, with recommendations that 'teachers should teach the whole class together for a high proportion of the lesson' (DfEE 1998, p. 19). A political assumption was being made that good practice could be handed over readymade and teachers were to become 'like technical operatives to receive packages of pedagogy from the outside which can be "read off" and "read in"' (Barber 2001, in Dadds 2001, p. 48). What has happened to the definition of education as 'giving access to the ideas and tools through which the learner's own distinctive personality might take place' (Pring 2004, p. 27)? That definition has been replaced by the current one which is 'utilitarian, represented in statutory curriculum documents and national requirements', an education process in which 'individuals are insignificant' (Goouch 2008, p. 93).

Pedagogy in 2010 has three paradigms and one result. Paradigm one is the accountancy model, beloved of policy makers nationally and internationally, and at the core of the school effectiveness debate (Gorard 2010). It is best defined as 'teach to be measured', in which the sole purpose of teaching is to cover material that will later be tested; there is no involvement of the pupil in that learning purpose. Paradigm two is the 'banking' model (Freire 1970), in which the teacher teaches and the pupils are taught; those are the fixed and regulated roles, there is no deregulation of the role (Perrenoud 1998). In 'olden days' this was known as the 'topping up' model, in which the child was the empty vessel and was topped up or filled up with knowledge which she recited back to the teacher to prove that learning had taken place (Alexander 2005, 2008; Tharp & Gallimore 1991, in Smith et al. 2004). Paradigm three is the 'testocracy' (Guinier & Torres 2003) in which the metric is laid down and the teaching and learning process conforms to that testing metric. The intended breadth and balance of the Education Reform Act 1988 has been lost within the dominance of the testocracy; the argument is not about the presence of a summative instrument – such an instrument has its place – but about that high-stakes instrument dominating pedagogy. Guinier & Torres assert that alongside the testocracy even the vagaries of teacher assessment stand out like a beacon of fairness and equity: 'reliance on teacher ratings excludes fewer people from lower socio-economic backgrounds than does reliance on test scores' (Guinier & Torres 2003, p. 71). The testocracy knows no boundaries but income, it even, as Guinier and Torres found in their research in the USA, redefines merit: 'it moved from an assumption that tests are meritocratic for everyone except people of colour to a larger critique of the way in which the conventional testocracy denies opportunity to many deserving white applicants as well. It changed the definition of merit' (2003, p. 72). It is important to remind ourselves what the introduction of this testocracy was meant to provide for the community: standardised tests and other objective measures of excellence were to enable administrators to compare individuals from different demographic, geographic and social cohorts. In a comparatively short time, the testing industry or performance measurement by testocracy has become established as the 'primary gatekeeper to upward mobility' (Guinier & Torres 2003).

Methodology

We wanted to explore whether using a guided group teaching strategy in a school with very high levels of social deprivation, indicated by Free School

Meals (FSM) and with 90 per cent English as an Additional Language (Ofsted Report, School A, March 2009) offered insights into Bernstein's socio-linguistic code theory. In essence, can the group which is being labelled as Bernstein's 'restricted code' population benefit from the treatment of a 'peda-gogy of plenty' to enable them to attain 'elaborated code' status? (Bernstein 1962a, 1962b, 1973).

Ofsted reported that 'children enter with skills much lower than what is typical for their age and many have delayed language and literacy skills with some not able to speak any English at all. Overall standards are well below average with weaknesses in communication, language and literacy and numeracy' (Ofsted report School A, March 2009, p. 5). We had carried out observations and conversations about practices of teaching and learning in the school for a full school year after the Ofsted report. The lesson which we report and analyse below is typical of the teaching and learning style in operation in teacher David's class throughout the year. David habitually used guided group strategies in his teaching.

We used an observation schedule adapted from Doyle (1987, pp. 93–96) and the coding frameworks of Galton et al. (1980) and Tizard et al. (1983) for descriptive analysis.

What is a guided group?

> It is a first principle for us that if you are teaching children as a whole class group, rather than planning your teaching and learning around individual learning needs, then you cannot be teaching formatively. If you teach without differentia-tion then how can you be matching learning to each child's developmental need? (Boyle & Charles 2008, p. 22)

This differentiated teaching philosophy was nested in the *Better Schools* report (DES 1985) and its four founding principles: 'broad, balanced, relevant and differentiated'. We feel that using the guided group strategy in a differ-entiated classroom 'balances learning needs common to all students with more specific needs tagged to individual learners' (Tomlinson 2001, p. 4). For McAdamis (2001) 'Differentiation allows the teacher to focus on the same key principles for all students, however the instructional process, the pace and rate towards understanding these concepts varies' (p. 3).

We define a guided group as always operating within a whole-class teach-ing structure, that is, moving from homogeneity to individualisation. The ses-sion will be focused on new learning or on consolidating a concept which the teacher feels the children have not internalised in their learning or on pursuing a learning sequence of stepped activities. The teacher has planned a number of differentiated learning activities within a teaching theme. Three out of the four groups will work independently (or with Teaching Assistant support) on those activities; the fourth group remains with the teacher and continues to be taught in the presence of the teacher, that group is the guided group. The duration of that focused uninterrupted teaching session for each guided group is approximately 20 minutes. The teacher plans a rota of guided group sessions to match and challenge the children's learning needs through-out the day and then develops the needs-related programme throughout the week.

Therefore, we agree with Williams's definition (2008) (see Chapter 6) in part but see a guided group offering four things to both teacher and child: a strategic (organisational) device; an optimal opportunity for specific and focused teaching; the small-group situation enables learning to be planned tightly and offers ready access to the teacher for the child; and finally it is the optimal opportunity for the teacher to focus her assessment obser-vations (of learning behaviours for example) with a group size of at most five children.

The theoretical underpinning of the guided group is encapsulated in Hayes's recognition that 'child-centred teaching includes behaviours that actively involve the children in guiding the learning process, such as offering choices, encouraging activity and suggesting solutions' (Hayes 2008, p. 433). In our work we have always believed that teaching is 'not a one-way process from the teacher to the child, it is a fluid, dynamic and often seemingly effort-less dance between teacher and child' (Matthews 1999, p. 162). Makin and Whiteman (2006) support this view in asserting that 'teachers and children are partners in teaching and learning transactions. We need to find ways of interacting with children to co-construct shared meanings in ways we cannot do if the children themselves are not active participants in exploring the situation' (p. 35).

How to plan a guided group: Looking at David's lesson

David worked with a guided group of five Year 1 children on a Design & Technology (D&T) activity. His D&T learning opportunities in this activity included: generating ideas (pupils learned how to make things to reduce noise to aid sleep); developing and communicating (pupils collaboratively planned types of headwear appliances that kept noise out); planning (Where do we start? How do we make the soundproof headwear? What will they look like?); evaluating (suitability of the product for effectiveness); developing their designing and making skills; nurturing creativity and innovation through designing and making.

The guided group session began with the teacher introducing the D&T theme through a read-aloud story (focused on Mr Bear, a story well known and well liked by the children). He involved the children in participating and talked through the purpose of the activity with all the children in a very detailed whole-class session. Following the whole-class presentation session, the class was organised into differentiated working groups. The guided group which David then taught worked out design solutions to the D&T problem in their own individual ways. The teacher was being carefully diverse as he had selected the composition of the guided group based on the children's problem-solving abilities. He deliberately selected a group which demonstrated a range of physical dexterities, confident oral contributions and high levels of creativity.

David's intention was to demonstrate focused assessment questioning based on identifying individual understanding of design problems. He wanted to strategically intervene to support each individual's thinking and his aim was that his formative pedagogy would encourage individuals to become independent co-constructors of learning. We were interested to see if David could carefully manage a balance of affective and cognitive development for the children. The opening of David's lesson is transcribed below.

David explored design ideas with the guided group to make headwear for Mr Bear to enable him to sleep through noise. He begins with the key design question: 'How are the ear pieces going to stay on Mr Bear's head?'

David:	Asafa have a look round here and see what you could use from here to take back. [Asafa is busy exploring the materials box and emerges with some small plastic lids and places them over and around both her ears.]
David:	Now you still need something to go over your head with the idea you have. Are you going to use flat ones like that? [Asafa nods in agreement 'Yeah'.]
David:	Now what are you going to use for the head part? [Asafa continues to root in the materials box and picks up a butter container.]
David:	Right you decide, you choose then.
Asafa:	I'll pick this one …
David:	Right you have got some ideas then. [David turns to another child who is holding up two empty yoghurt pots.]
David:	Amina, now how are you going to get these to stay on your ears?
Amina:	Erm, I, I …
David:	Could we not make it easier for him? How can we make it easier for him? How are we going to get them onto his head without falling off? Sellotape them onto his head or sellotape them onto something else.
Amina:	I know, I know, child responds to David's question. We could sellotape on here. [Asafa points to his set of materials including yoghurt pots, cardboard tube, glue.]
David:	Right, are you telling me, Asafa that he's going to have to spend all night holding them on to his head like this?
Asafa:	No.

David: Right then. [David holds up the plastic pots]. How are we going to fix them onto something.

Asafa: Glue.

Maryam: Like this sir [holds up yoghurt pots on either end of a cardboard tube].

David: [Ignoring Maryam] I don't think he'd like glue on his head Asafa. Gluing them onto his head, I don't think he'd like that.

          [Maryam holds up her suggestion again.]

David   Now how is that going to work Maryam? How is that going to keep the
replies: noise out of his ears? Those ear muffs that I brought into school, how did they work?

Maryam: You could put the tube on top of it.

David: Show me how that is going to work. [Maryam now changes the position of the pots from the end of tube to underneath the tube.]

David: Mmmm. How is that going to work Maryam? How did my ear muffs work? How did they stay on my head?

Analysis and discussion

We can see that David has recognised the importance of these 'organisational and instructional changes' as a move away from the dominance of whole-class teaching (DCSF 2007a). He understands that a guided group is not, as Williams states (2008), 'an organisational approach where attention is given to children who require additional support' (p. 67). David knows that using a guided group teaching strategy is *not* a special needs support strategy.

David also demonstrates that 'if you are teaching children as a whole class group, rather than planning your teaching and learning around individual learning needs, then you cannot be teaching formatively. If you teach without differentiation then how can you be matching learning to each child's developmental need?' (Boyle & Charles 2008, p. 22). The children were sufficiently motivated by David to enable them to produce individual design ideas and subsequently products in a move away from 'one-size-fits-all' homogeneity.

However, through Bernstein's perspective (1962a, 1973), closer analysis of David's language code (evidenced by the transcript) suggests his pedagogy is that of the restricted code rather than the elaborated code. Analysis of David's strong control of the language transactions, almost monologic, and certainly not dialogic in any shape or form, indicated that David's perception of his pupils and their abilities is firmly rooted in the Ofsted analysis. Note the labelling language used in the report: 'a school with very high levels of social deprivation, Free School Meals (FSM) and with 90% English as an Additional Language' (Ofsted Report, School A, March 2009). We felt that David's confused attempt to introduce a guided group philosophy offered some insights into Bernstein's socio-linguistic code theory. How could the guided group with whom David is working and which is being labelled as Bernstein's 'restricted code' population, benefit from the treatment of a 'pedagogy of plenty' (Haberman 1981) to enable them to attain 'elaborated code' status? (Bernstein 1962a, 1962b, 1973). Firstly, David has failed to change the regulation in the learning process between himself and his pupils (Perrenoud 1998). He has assumed the traditional role of power (Bernstein 1970) in which he asks the questions and hence structures the children's thinking. The illusion of formativeness is maintained through the group set-up and the relatively free movement of the children to and from the materials. However, from analysis of the transcript of the working session, it is evident from the representative section set out below that David even controls the materials selected, by challenging the pupils' choices of materials and design. Read, for example, the opening section of the transcript for the continual uninterrupted question sequences; there is not one question framed by a child in this section of the transcript. David is taking the position of control and indicating to the children that he is the problem solver and they are the recipients of instructions which they then carry out to produce quite firmly controlled outcomes.

The children are struggling to find a solution, for example a band to connect the ear pieces, so David pursues this with:

David:	How did my ear muffs work? How did they stay on my head? How did my ear muffs stay on that I was using? I did not have to hold them on with my hands like that.
Safia:	No, no …
David:	But why did they not fall off?
Safia:	Because you have a big head.
David:	I have got a very big head Safia but it was not just my big head that kept my ear muffs on was it?
Safia:	No.
David:	How did they stay on my head?
Amina interjects and replies:	I know. You had a band on your head.
David:	That's right I had a big pink band across my head to keep it on my head.
David:	Right Safia, you have got plenty of feathers there. I want you to tell me how it is going to stay on my head first.
	[Maryam comes over with a large straw and hands it to David.]

David:	How is that going to work? Go on and show me. [Hands straw back to Maryam. Maryam turns a yoghurt pot upside down and places the straw across the bottom.]
David:	Mmm. Is that going to be strong enough Maryam or is that going to break? Do you think we need something stronger? [Maryam bends the straw to see if it does break. It doesn't.]
David:	It is going to break isn't it? Go and see if there is something stronger. Maryam, What can we use to make a band? What can we use to make a band go round your head?
Maryam:	A bubble ... a bubble.

It is even more noticeable from the full transcript that David's style of interaction has limited rather than enhanced the children's responses. In fact, his pedagogical style has put limits on the children's collaborative learning, preventing any dialogic enquiry or cooperative exploration. His questions 'do not cognitively challenge the child' (Siraj-Blatchford & Manni 2008, p. 13) and his questions dominate the session in quantity rather than quality, 'demanding only simple recall' (p. 13). Maryam's response, by gesture, is typical of the group; for example Maryam bends the straw but does not say anything in response. Inadvertently, David is embodying the 'restricted code' in full. He expects no language in response to his constant questions and is sadly rewarded by getting none. He does not self-evaluate and modify his own behaviour; see, for example the following sequence of questions directed without pause to Maryam and the other children:

| **David:** | Have you ever made one from that [leather] in school? Maybe we could have a look for some? [Maryam runs off to resource area to find some leather.] Do you want to come and look for some because you are going to have to put it around your head? [David is addressing the rest of the group.] That won't break, come and have a look. [Motions again to the rest of the group to put down the materials they are working with. Children continue working.] Maryam come over here. [Maryam returns empty handed.] Now I think Amina's [model] might work, let's go and find something that you are going to need Asafa that will keep it on his head otherwise it will fall off. Safia I want you to leave ... come on, put those feathers on [Maryam and Asafa go off with David to the resource area.] What about things like this then? [David holds up a long strip of material.] Which way does it go? [Asafa demonstrates long pieces hanging down like ears.] |

Analysis of the full transcript reveals that of the 107 oral transactions in the 21-minute session, David made 60 of these. This approximates to teacher-speak every 20 seconds of the session. Even at this level, the balance of transactions between one voice (teacher) and four children (Asafa, Maryam, Safia and Amina) is inequitable. However, on analysis, David's 60 contributions actually contain 112 questions or direct instructions, a dominance of the session which shuts down the 'principal means by which pupils actively engage and constructively intervene through talk' (Alexander 2004, p. 12). The four children respond as follows: Asafa 9 responses, Amina 11, Maryam 15 and Safia 7. Without exception these responses are all short, do not engage in exploration of problem solving in the design and technology context and are very limited in terms of cognitive interrogatives. In plain statistical terms, the children only respond to about a third of David's questions – in many cases largely because he either does not allow them sufficient time to respond or because they are used to his pedagogical style of a discourse in which the teacher is dominant (Alexander 2008; Allal & Ducrey 2000; Freire 1970). In short, David has 'restricted' not just the opportunities for dialogue and dialogic (Wells 2001b) but the potential for collaborative exploration of the design and technology process. David's low percentage (5%) of open questions compares 'poorly with the 9.9% of open questions used by key stage 2 teachers in the ORACLE primary school study, already disappointingly low' (Galton et al. 1999a, p. 29). David's percentage correlates closely with Siraj-Blatchford & Manni's REPEY Study (2008) which found that '94.5% of all the questions asked by staff were closed questions that required a recall of fact, experience or expected behaviour, decision between a limited selection of choices or no response at all' (p. 5).

Conclusion

We wanted to explore whether using a guided group teaching strategy in a school with very high levels of social deprivation and indicated by Free School Meals (FSM) and with 90 per cent of children having English as an Additional Language (Ofsted Report, School A, March 2009), offered insights into Bernstein's socio-linguistic code theory. Significant questions about David's pedagogy arose once the transcript of the guided group session was analysed. How much was David influenced by the Ofsted labelling of his school and in consequence how much did it affect his restrictive pedagogical style? Can David's guided group benefit from the treatment of a 'pedagogy of plenty' (Haberman 1991) to enable them to attain 'elaborated code' status? (Bernstein 1962a, 1962b, 1973). The lesson proved to be a cautionary tale. Guided group work is a necessary platform to enable that 'pedagogy of plenty', that is, good teaching and learning. The interaction between curriculum, assessment and teaching/learning methods or pedagogy, for example guided group work, is fundamental, and 'attempts to change one and not the other are likely to lead to frustration and failure' (Weston 1992, p. 8). The teacher should carefully plan the independent activities and the guided group work to maintain challenge and interest levels. 'The teacher has a central role in making group work more effective and developing pupils' group-working skills' (Blatchford et al. 2003, p. 13). It is important for the teacher to find time for the formative observation of children, and the guided group situation provides an optimal opportunity to observe learning behaviours as well as development stages of outputs. The teacher also needs to acquire the skill of structuring lessons carefully to facilitate learning in groups. 'We recommend that all lessons that involve group-work should include briefing and debriefing to enhance reflection and help develop learning. The aim is to help pupils as well as teachers become meta-cognitively wise about group working' (Blatchford et al. 2002, p. 13).

Teacher intervention can induce superficial compliance on the part of the pupil to 'the didactic contract of the instructional activity without allowing genuine developmental progress in the construction of cognitive, conative and social competencies' (Allal & Ducrey 2000, p. 149). David's practice demonstrates this didactic contract even within the context of a guided group teaching setting; the children have become so indoctrinated by David's pedagogy that their possibilities for exploration have become diminished, even within the guided group in which support and development should be optimal (Boyle & Charles 2010b). David's pedagogy is dictated by, according to Labov (1969), his 'notion of the myth of verbal deprivation on the part of working class children' (in Tizard et al. 1983, p. 533). The study which Tizard et al. carried out with 40 children on the complex uses of language at home and at school produced 'significant differences in teacher's talk in which the inhibiting effect of the teachers on working class children was also apparent in other aspects of their language development' (Tizard et al. 1983, p. 539). From their transcript there is clear 'significant social class difference in the teacher's talk, with more complex uses being addressed to middle class children than to working class children' (Tizard et al. 1983, p. 537).

This case study demonstrates the dominant paradigm of a 'pedagogy of poverty' (Hodges 2001) with its 95 per cent of closed questions and the assumption by the teacher that the children are only capable of being exposed to the 'restricted code' (Bernstein 1970) at the expense of a 'pedagogy of plenty' (Haberman 1991). Bernstein's theory of classification (power) and framing (control) of education knowledge (Bernstein 1970) is overtly practised in English classrooms (Alexander 2005, 2008; Boyle & Charles 2010a). This 'pedagogy of poverty' is now practised in the current 'one-size-fits-all' model (Alexander 2005, 2008; Myhill 2006; Wyse 2007) of teaching and learning operating within the agencies of accountability and the 'testocracy' (Guinier & Torres 2003). At government policy level there needs to be an acknowledgement of this situation, as evidenced by the REPEY findings (Siraj-Blatchford & Manni 2008). One small step, six years ago in the Primary National Strategy, was the statement of one of the Key

Elements of Effective Practice (KEEP) as: 'the importance of the practitioner's role in sustained shared thinking and the kinds of interactions that will guide but not dominate children's thinking' (DfES 2005, p. 10).

CHAPTER 9

CONCLUDING THOUGHTS

We stated in our Introduction that the principal theme of this book was to be an exploration of the process of developing young readers and writers through non-traditional means. To achieve this, we set out to demonstrate, illustrate and critique approaches to teaching through the use of multiliteracies (which we exemplified through fiction, expository/instructions, poetry, recount) and multimodalities (similarly through reading, writing, speaking, listening, performing, illustrating). Our aim was to present material which in the first instance would interest the reader/practitioner and hopefully provoke reflection and support the trainee/current teacher/researcher in understanding how to address and 'scaffold' the complex needs of a learner with depth and breadth. A commissioned report on behalf of the National Council for Curriculum and Assessment by Kennedy et al. (2012) built on a broad conceptualisation of the early work of Debes and recognises the importance of multiple modes and multiple representations in literacy. It also defines literacy from a semiotic position to include linguistic and non-linguistic forms of communication (Kennedy et al. 2012, p. 54).

We started from the premise in our research that, as formative thinkers and practitioners, we recognise the central importance of formative assessment in the process of effective teaching and learning and our aim is to build practitioners' understanding and capacity to use formative assessment as an integral component in that process. Despite the strategies, myths and gimmicks that have been operationalised in its name, formative assessment is a simple concept. To borrow a quotation from Philippe Perrenoud: 'Any assessment that helps a pupil to learn and develop is formative' (1991, p. 80). It is important that teachers know and understand how formative assessment helps the pupil to learn and how feedback from assessment supports that learning process.

In our understanding of the literature, a teacher's main role is to try to understand and support the learner on his/her journey to becoming an autonomous literate individual. Three key issues have emerged in our practical work and research – complexity, content knowledge and individual progression, and these three issues need application in the classroom situation to the 'real world' of the young learner seeking automaticity. For example, this can be achieved by introducing a multimodal aspect to the act of teaching, such as understanding how socio-dramatic play can support the emergent writer or how young communicators can support each other in narrative construction. Our philosophy is that teaching and learning and assessment evidences are mutually co-dependent and progress in learning depends to a large extent on the authentic involvement of the pupil in the learning process. Within the domain of writing development, we recognise and deconstruct for the trainee/current teacher the complexity of this process, based on easing the cognitive load. This can be achieved by reducing the current unrealistic learning outcomes (expectations) caused by applying a 'one-size-fits-all' generalisation across a heterogeneous (classroom cohort) group to bring about a homogeneous learning outcome. How can these aims be achieved?

By supporting teachers to develop the understanding and use of various strategies (such as eliciting evidence, analysis and action) we intend that trainees/teachers will see the need to become more effective in identifying and using evidence to provide meaningful, relevant and progressive activities matched to individual learning interests and needs.

We saw the need for this book based on our classroom research (Boyle & Charles 2010a), which was based on observations and interviews with a representative national sample of primary school teachers and their understanding and operational use of Assessment for Learning. The research produced evidence of limited training in, and understanding, of learning steps, learning trajectories (Heritage 2011) and progressions, especially within the domain of early literacy. We anticipated supporting formative teaching for deeper learning through the use in the book of concrete examples illustrated through case studies and step-by-step commentary. For example, the oft quoted but mainly misunderstood concept of 'scaffolding' is addressed through modelling for the teacher on how to 'scaffold' a child struggling with the alphabet to write a decodable sentence independently through semiotics, pictures and other signs. Similarly, 'scaffolding' is a required strategy for the child who is regarded as 'able' but requires support to develop more higher-order skills, and modelling of alternative experiences and strategies for deeper, richer learning is needed for the groups of children who 'get by' through disappearing into the 'acceptable level' category of the current measurement model.

We have tried to exemplify issues such as how to 'scaffold' for the range of children's needs within the different language demands of the genres of poetry, narrative, expository texts, fantasy and recount. One example illustrates the developmental process for the child progressing from a first-person account and connecting back to her reading material and making those transferable connections to what she has written. The primacy of the processes of multimodality and multiliteracies in emerging literacy development are established. For example, themes such as the value to the learner of oral rehearsal leading to growth in aspects of literacy, are never de-contextualised and are always presented in an embedded, realistic way to the reader or learner. The book excludes a focus on product, outcomes, that is, scores, levels, percentages, etc. but focuses on 'how' the child becomes a competent user of language, moving towards the goals of self-regulated learning and automaticity then the journey to becoming a lifelong learner.

Children and their learning interests are at the centre of this book just as they have to be at the centre of all schools' language development programmes. The book focuses on the core pedagogical issues such as the integration of teaching, learning and assessment; the crucial teacher-centred vs child-centred debate; didactic (transmission model) teaching vs formative (transactional learner-centred) teaching; homogeneity vs heterogeneity; and the pressures on learner-centred teaching of an accountability policy agenda.

We address major issues for successful language development and rich teaching pedagogy. These include the integration of modes of language development; immersion in types/modes of story, rhyme; teacher understanding of the importance of lessening the cognitive load and the implications of overloading 'working memory' for the learner, interest levels, motivation and commitment; relevance for the learner; in short, the importance of supporting the learner's affective domain and balancing the importance given to tests of cognition (understanding the triangulation and integration of cognitive, affective, conative domains on effective learning); and finally being sensitive to micro but vital developmental concerns for the young learner such as physicality (e.g. motor control, pencil grip, pacing, task completion, etc.).

We are aware of and do not underestimate the pressures teachers face in developing creativity and creative experiences for children while competing for space against current accountability and 'topical' political agendas, (current example, phonics groups/testing) but we hope that the book has caused thinking, a period of reflection and possibly some changes in practice.

REFERENCES

Alexander RJ (2004) *Towards Dialogic Teaching: Rethinking Classroom Talk*. York: Dialogos.

Alexander RJ (2005) Culture, dialogue and learning: Notes on an emerging pedagogy. Paper presented at International Association for Cognitive Education and Psychology Conference, July, Durham, UK.

Alexander RJ (2008) *Education For All, the Quality Imperative and the Problem of Pedagogy*. Pathways to Access Research Monograph No. 20. Create: Consortium for Research on Educational Access, Transitions and Equity, Institute of Education, University of London.

Alexander RJ & Flutter J (2009) *Towards a New Primary Curriculum: A Report from the Cambridge Primary Review. Part 1: Past and Present*. Cambridge: University of Cambridge Faculty of Education.

Allal L & Ducrey GP (2000) Assessment of – or in – the zone of proximal development. *Learning & Instruction* 10: 137–152.

Allal L & Lopez L (2005) *Formative Assessment of Learning: A Review of Publications in French*. Paris: OECD.

Allal L, Lopez L, Lehraus K & Forget A (2005) *Whole Class & Peer Interaction in an Activity of Writing and Revision*. In: Kostouli T (ed.) *Writing in Contexts: Textual Practices and Learning Processes in Socio-cultural Settings*. New York: Springer, pp. 69–91.

Andrzejczak N, Trainin G & Poldberg M (2005) From image to text: Using images in the writing process. *International Journal of Education & the Arts* 6(12): 1–17. Available at: http://www.ijea.org/v6n12/v6n12.pdf

Applebee A (1978) *The Child's Concept of Story: Ages Two to Seventeen*. Chicago, IL: University of Chicago Press.

Arapaki X & Zafrana M (2004) The artistic expression of kindergarten children after a 'guided' teaching approach. *European Early Childhood Education Research Journal* 12(2): 43–57.

Ausburn L & Ausburn F (1978) *Visual Literacy: Background, Theory and Practice. PLET* 15(4): 291–297.

Baines E, Blatchford P & Chowne A (2007) Improving the effectiveness of collaborative group work in primary schools: effects on science attainment. *British Educational Research Journal* 33(5): 663–680.

Bamford A (2003) *The Visual Literacy White Paper*. Australia: Art and Design University of Technology, Sydney.

Banks JA (1994) Transforming the mainstream curriculum. *Educating for Diversity* 51(8): 4–8.

Beale AM (2013) Skimming and scanning: Two important strategies for speeding up your reading. Available at: http://www.howtolearn.com/2013/02/skimming-and-scanning-two-important-strategies-for-speeding-up-your-reading/

Beaman A (1999) Collaborative writing K-12. Available at: http://castle.eiu.edu/~rhetoric/anthology/collab/secondary.htm

Bean W & Bouffler C (1987) *Spell by Writing*. Australia: Australian Print Group.

Beck IL & McKeown, MG (1996) Questioning the author: A yearlong classroom implementation to engage students with text. *The Elementary School Journal* 96: 385–415.

Beck IL & McKeown MG (2001) Text talk: Capturing the benefits of read-aloud experiences for young children. *The Reading Teacher* 55(1): 10–20.

Becker A (2004) A review of writing model research based on cognitive processes. In: Horning A & Becker A (eds) *Revision: History, Theory & Practice*. Santa Barbara: University of California.

Bereiter C & Scardamalia M (1987) *The Psychology of Written Composition*. Hillsdale, NJ: Lawrence Erlbaum.

Bereiter C & Scardamalia M (1996) Rethinking learning. In: Olson DR & Torrance N (eds) *The Handbook of Education and Human Development: New Models of Teaching, Learning and Schooling*. Cambridge, MA: Basil Blackwell, pp. 485–513.

Berninger V (1995) Introduction. In: Berninger V (ed.) *The varieties of orthographic knowledge II: Relationships to phonology, reading and writing*. Dordrecht, the Netherlands: Kluwer Academic, pp. 1–22.

Berninger V (2001) *Process Assessment of the Learner (PAL) – Test Battery For Reading and Writing*. San Antonio, TX: PsychCorp/Harcourt.

Berninger V, Abbott RD, Jones J, Wolf BJ, Gould L, Anderson-Youngstrom M, Shaimada S & Apel K (2006) Early development of language by hand: Composing, reading, listening and speaking connections: Three letter-writing modes and fast mapping in spelling. *Developmental Neuropsychology* 29(1): 61–92.

Bernstein B (1962a) Linguistic codes, hesitation phenomena and intelligence. *Language and Speech* 5(1): 31–46.

Bernstein B (1962b) Social class, linguistic codes and grammatical elements. *Language and Speech* 5(4): 221–240.

Bernstein B (1970) Education cannot compensate for society. *New Society* 15(387): 344–347.

Bernstein B (1973) *Class, Codes and Control, Vol. 1*. London: Routledge & Kegan Paul.

Bernstein B (1996) *Pedagogy, Symbolic Control and Identity: Theory, Research, Critique*. London: Taylor & Francis.

Blatchford P, Kutnick P, Baines E & Galton (2003) *Paper for Special Edition of International Journal of Educational Research*. pp. 1–19.

Blatchford P, Baines E, Rubie-Davis C, Bassatt P & Chowne A (2006) The effect of a new approach to group work on pupil–pupil and teacher–pupil interactions. *Journal of Educational Psychology* 98(4): 750–765.

Blatchford P, Kutnick P & Baines E (2007) Pupil grouping for learning in classroom: Results from the UK SPRinG study. Paper presented at American Educational Research Annual Meeting, Chicago.

Blatchford P, Kutnick P, Baines E & Galton M (2003) Towards a social pedagogy of classroom group work. *International Journal of Educational Research* 39: 153–172.

Boaler J (2005) The 'psychological prison' from which they never escaped: the role of ability grouping in reproducing social class inequalities. *FORUM* 47(2–3): 135–144.

Bourke L & Adams A (2010) Cognitive constraints and the early learning goals in writing. *Journal of Research in Reading* 33(1): 94–110.

Boyle B & Bragg J (2006) A curriculum without foundation. *British Educational Research Journal* 32(4): 569–582.

Boyle B & Bragg J (2008) Making primary connections: The cross curriculum story. *The Curriculum Journal* 19(1): 3–18.

Boyle B & Bragg J (2009) What a waste of money! *The Educational Journal*. No. 114, 9(4): 44–47.

Boyle B & Charles M (2008) Are we doing it right? A review of the assessment for learning strategy. *Primary Leadership Today* 2(14): 20–24.

Boyle B & Charles M (2009) Formative assessment of teaching and learning in primary classrooms. *International Journal of Learner Diversity* 1(1): 17–34.

Boyle B & Charles M (2010a) Leading learning through assessment for learning. *School Leadership & Management* 30(3): 285–300.

Boyle B & Charles M (2010b) Using socio-dramatic play to support a beginning writer: Daniel, the doctor and the bleeding ball. *Early Years Education* 18(3): 213–225.

Boyle B & Charles M (2011) Re-defining assessment: The struggle to ensure a balance between accountability and comparability based on a 'testocracy' and the development of humanistic individuals through assessment. Special; issue of CADMO: *An International Journal of Educational Research* 19(1): 55–65.

Boyle B & Charles M (2012) David, Mr Bear and Bernstein: searching for an equitable pedagogy through guided group work. *The Curriculum Journal* 23(1): 117–133.

Brehony KJ (2005) Primary schooling under New Labour. *Oxford Review of Education* 31(1): 29–46.

Browne A (2000) *Gorilla*. London: Walker.

Bruner J (1983) *Child's Talk: Learning to Use Language*. New York: Norton.

Bruner J (1990) *Acts of Meaning*. Cambridge London: Harvard University Press.

Bruning R & Horn C (2000) Developing motivation to write. *Educational Psychologist* 35(1): 25–37.

Bullock Report (1975) *A Language for Life*, DES. HMSO: London.

Burkard T (2004) *After the Literacy Hour: May the Best Plan Win*. London: Centre for Policy Studies.

Callow J (2008) Show me: Principles for assessing students' visual literacy. *The Reading Teacher* 61(8): 616–626.

Carey A, Wolf A & Mieras EL (1996) What is this Literachurch stuff anyway? Pre-service teachers' growth in understanding children's literary responses. *Reading Research Quarterly* 31(2): 130–157.

Carolan J & Guinn A (2007) Differentiation: Lessons from master teachers. *Educational Leadership. Improving Instruction for Students with Learning Needs* 64(5): 44–47.

Cassell J, Ryokai K & Vaucelle C (2002) Literacy learning by storytelling with a virtual peer. Proceedings of computer support for collaborative learning. January 7-11 *Boulder* CO, pp. 352–360.

Chalker S & Weiner E (1998) *Oxford Dictionary of English Grammar*. Oxford: Oxford University Press.

Chapman JW & Turner WE (2003) Reading difficulties, reading-related self perceptions and strategies for overcoming negative self-beliefs. *Reading & Writing Quarterly* 19: 15–24.

Christie J (1991) *Play and Early Literacy Development*. Albany, NY: University of New York Press.

Christie J & Roskos K (2001) Examining the play–literacy interface: A critical review and future directions. *Journal of Early Childhood Literacy* 1(1): 59–89.

Clark JM & Paivio A (1991) Dual Coding Theory and Education. *Educational Psychology Review* 3(3): 148–210.

Clarke LK (1988) Invented versus traditional spelling in first graders' writing: Effects on learning to spell and read. *Research in the Teaching of English* 22: 281–309.

Coffey J, Hammer D, Levin DM and Grant T (2011) The missing disciplinary substance of formative assessment. *Journal of Research in Science Teaching* 48(10): 1109–36.

Cook M (2000) Writing and role play: A case for inclusion. *Reading* 34(2): 74–78.

Corden R (2007) Developing reading-writing connections: the impact of explicit instruction of literary devices of the quality of children's narrative writing. *Journal of Research in Childhood Education*. Spring, 21(3): 1–15.

Cowie H & Rudduck J (1988) *Learning Together – Working Together. Co-operative Group Work – an Overview (Vol. 1)*. London: BP Educational Service.

Crooks T (1988) *Assessing Student Performance*. Kensington, Australia: Higher Education Research & Development Society of Australia.

Curtis A & Bailey KM (2001) Picture your students talking: Using pictures in the language classroom. *ESL Magazine* 4(4): 10–11.

Czerniewska P (1992) *Learning About Writing: The Early Years*. Oxford: Blackwell.

Dadds M (2001) The politics of pedagogy. *Teachers and Teaching: Theory and Practice* 7(1): 43–58.

Danzig A (1995) Applications and distortions of Basil Bernstein's code. In: Sadovnik AR (ed.) *Knowledge and Pedagogy: The Sociology of Basil Bernstein*. Norwood, NJ: Ablex Publishing, pp.145–170.

Dauite C & Dalton B (1993) Collaboration between children learning to write: Can novices be masters? *Cognition & Instruction* 10(4): 281–333.

DCSF (2007a) *Early Years Foundation Stage*. London: DCSF.

DCSF (2007b) *Improving Writing With a Focus on Guided Writing. Leading Improvement Using the Primary Framework*. London: DCSF. Ref: 00618-2007BKT-EN

Debes J (1968) Some foundations of visual literacy. *Audio Visual Instruction* 13: 961–964.

Delisi R (2002) From marbles to instant messenger: Implications of Piaget's ideas about peer learning. *Theory into Practice* 41(1): 5–12.

Depree H & Iverson S (1994) *Early Literacy in the Classroom*. Western Australia: Wright Group Publishing.

DES (1985) *Better Schools: A Summary*. Department of Education and Science and Welsh Office, March 1985. London: Her Majesty's Stationery Office.

DfEE (1997) *Excellence for All Children*. London: The Stationery Office.

DfEE (1998) *National Literacy Strategy: Framework for Teaching*. London: DfEE.

DfEE (1999) *National Numeracy Strategy: Framework for Teaching*. London: DfEE.

DfEE (2001) *Developing Early Writing*. London: DfEE.

DfES (2005) *Primary National Strategy Key Elements of Effective Practice (KEEP)*. DfES/SureStart: London.

Doyle JR (1987) Classification by ordering a sparse matrix. *Journal of Applied Mathematical Modelling* 12(1): 86–94.

Draper D (2012) *Comprehension Strategies: Visualising and Visual Literacy*. Northern Adelaide Region Comprehension Focus.

Duffield J & Peacock C (2000) Learning to write. *Research in Education*. 65(Winter): 1–4.

Dufflemeyer BB & Ellertson A (2005) Critical visual literacy: Multimodal communication across the curriculum. Across the disciplines: Interdisciplinary perspectives on language, learning & academic writing. Available at: http://wac.colostate.edu/atd/visual/dufflemeyer_ellerston.cfm (June 2008).

Duke NK (2000) 3.6 minutes per day: The scarcity of informational texts in first grade. *Reading Research Quarterly* 35: 202–224.

Duke NK & Kays J (1998) 'Can I say "once upon a time?"': Kindergarten children developing knowledge of information book language. *Early Childhood Research Quarterly* 13: 295–318.

Dunsmuir S & Blatchford P (2004) Predictors of writing competence in 4–7 year old children. *British Journal of Educational Psychology* 47: 461–483.

Education Department, Western Australia (1997) *Writing: Developmental Continuum.* Australia: Heinemann.

Ehri LC (1992) Reconceptualising the development of sight word reading and its relationship to recoding. In: Gough P, Ehri LC & Treiman R (eds) *Reading Acquisition.* Hillsdale, NJ: Erlbaum, pp. 107–143.

Ehri LC (1995) Phases of development in learning to read words by sight. *Journal of Research in Reading* 18: 116–125.

Ehri L & Metsala J (1998) *Word Recognition in Beginning Literacy.* London: Paul Chapman.

Eke R & Lee J (2004) Pace and differentiation in the literacy hour: Some outcomes of an analysis of transcripts. *The Curriculum Journal* 15(3): 219–231.

Emig J (1971*) The Composing Processes of 12th Graders.* NCTE Research Report 13.

Englert S, Mariage TV & Dunsmore K (2006) Tenets of sociocultural theory in writing research. In: MacArthur CA, Graham S & Fitzgerald J (eds) *Handbook of Writing Research.* New York: The Guilford Press, pp. 208–221.

Eraut M (1994) *Developing Professional Knowledge and Competence.* London: Falmer Press.

Ernst K (1994) *Picturing Learning.* Portsmouth, NH: Heinemann.

Feez S (1998) *Text-based Syllabus Design.* Sydney: McQuarie University/AMES.

Fenwick G (1990) *Teaching Children's Literature in the Primary School.* London: David Fulton Publishers.

Fisher R & Williams M (2000) *Unlocking Literacy: A Guide for Teachers.* London: David Fulton.

Flower L (1989) *Problem-solving Strategies for Writing* (3rd edition) New York: Harcourt College Publishers.

Flower L, Hayes JR, Carey L, Schriver K & Stratman J (1986) Detection, diagnosis and the strategies of revision. *College Composition and Communication* 37(1): 16–53.

Fox C (1993) *At the Very Edge of the Forest: The Influence of Literature on Storytelling by Children.* London: Cassell.

Francis B (2011) A different class of cleverness. *Times Educational Supplement Magazine* 22 July, pp. 6–16.

Frater G (2004) Improving Dean's writing: Or, shall we tell the children? *Literacy* 38(2): 78–82.

Freire P (1970) *Pedagogy of the Oppressed.* Harmondsworth: Penguin.

Fresch MJ (2007) Teachers' concerns about spelling instruction: a national survey. *Reading Psychology* 28(4): 301–330.

Galton M (1990) Grouping and Groupwork. In Rogers C & Kutnick P (eds) *The Social Psychology of the Primary School.* London: Routledge.

Galton M & Hargreaves L (2009) Group work: Still a neglected art? *Cambridge Journal of Education* 39(1): 1–6.

Galton M, Hargreaves L, Comber C, Wall D & Pell A (1999a) *Inside the Primary Classroom: 20 Years On.* London: Routledge.

Galton M, Hargreaves L, Comber C, Wall D & Pell T (1999b) Changes in patterns of teacher interaction in primary classrooms: 1976–96. *British Educational Research Journal* 25(1): 23–37.

Galton M, Simon B & Croll P (1980) *Inside the Primary Classroom.* London: Routledge & Kegan Paul.

Galton M, Hargreaves L, Comber C, Wall D & Pell T (1999) Changes in patterns of teacher interaction in primary classrooms: 1976–1996. *British Educational Research Journal,* 25(1): 23–37.

Gambrell LB & Jawitz PB (1993) Mental Imagery, Text Illustrations and children's Story comprehension and Recall. *Reading Research Quarterly* 28(3): 264–276.

Gamble N & Yates S (2002) *Exploring Children's Literature: Teaching the Language and Reading of Fiction*. London: Paul Chapman.

Gammage P (1987) Chinese whispers. *Oxford Review of Education* 13(1): 95–109.

Gardner H (1991) *The Unschooled Mind: How Children Think and How Schools Should Teach*. New York: Basic Books.

Gentry R (1982) An analysis of developmental spelling in GNYS AT WRK. *The Reading Teacher* 36(2): 192–200.

Gibbons A (2001) Boy trouble. *The Teacher* (November), p. 16–17.

Goouch K (2008) Understanding playful pedagogies, play narratives and play spaces. *Early Years: An International Journal of Research and Development* 28(1): 93–102.

Gorard S (2010) Serious doubts about school effectiveness. *British Educational Research Journal* 36(5): 745–766.

Graham S & Harris KR (2000) The role of self-regulation and transcription skills in writing and writing development. *Educational Psychologist* 35(1): 3–12.

Graham S & Perin D (2007) *Writing Next: Effective Strategies to Improve the Writing of Adolescents in Middle and High Schools. A Report to Carnegie Corporation of New York*. Washington, DC: Alliance for Excellent Education.

Graham S, Harris KR & Mason L (2005) Improving the writing performance, knowledge, and self-efficacy of struggling young writers: The effects of self-regulated strategy development. *Contemporary Educational Psychology* 30: 207–241.

Graham S & Hebert M (2010) *Writing to Read: Evidence for How Writing can Improve Reading*. A report from Carnegie Corporation of New York. Vanderbilt University.

Graves DH (1983) *Writing: Teachers and Children at Work*. Portsmouth, NH: Heinemann.

Graves DH (1994) *A Fresh Look at Writing*. Portsmouth, NH: Heinemann.

Guinier L & Torres G (2003) *The Miner's Canary: Enlisting Race, Resisting Power, Transforming Democracy*. Cambridge, MA: Harvard University Press.

Haberman M (1991) The pedagogy of poverty versus good teaching. *Phi Delta Kappan* December: 290–294.

Haley D (1999) Collaborative writing: Some late 20th century trends. Available at: http://www.etsu.edu/haleyd/essay2collab.html

Hall N (1991) *Writing With Reason: The Emergence of Authorship in Young Children*. London: Hodder & Stoughton.

Hall N & Robinson A (1998) *Exploring Writing and Play in the Early Years*. London: David Fulton Press.

Harrett J (2002) Young children talking: An investigation into the personal stories of Key Stage One Infants. *Early Years* 22(1): 19–26.

Hartley D (1993) *Understanding the Nursery School*. London: Cassell.

Hartley D (2002) Global influences on teacher education. *Journal of Education for Teaching* 28(3): 78–105.

Hartman DK (2002) *Using Information Books in the Classroom: Letting the Facts (and Research) Speak for Themselves*. Red Brick Learning, pp. 1–20.

Harvey S (2002) Nonfiction inquiry: Using real reading and writing to explore the world. *Language Arts* 80(1): 12–22.

Hayes N (2008) Teaching matters in early educational practice: The case for a nurturing pedagogy. *Early Education and Development* 19(3): 430–440.

Heald-Taylor G (1998) Three paradigms of spelling instruction in Grades 3–6. *The Reading Teacher* 51(5): 404–413.

Heritage M (2011) Knowing what to do next: The hard part of formative assessment. *CADMO* 19(1): 67–84.

Heydon R (2007) Making meaning together: Multimodal literacy learning opportunities in an inter-generational art programme. *Journal of Curriculum Studies* 39(1): 35–62.

Hibbert L (2009) Tracing the benefits of multimodal learning in a self-portrait project in Mitchell's Plain, South Africa. *Southern African Linguistics & Applied Language Studies* 27(2): 203–213.

Hibbing AN & Rankin-Erickson JL (2003) A picture is worth a thousand words: Using visual images to improve comprehension for middle school struggling readers. *The Reading Teacher*, 56(8): 758–770.

Hochman W (2002) Using paired fiction writing: Transactional creativity and community building in the composition class. Available at: www.southernct.edu/~hochman/Willsedessay

Hodges G (2002) Learning through collaborative writing. *Reading, Literacy and Language* 36(1): 4–10.

Hodges H (2001) Overcoming a pedagogy of power. In: Cole R (ed.) *More Strategies for Educating Everybody's Children*. Alexandria, VA: ASCD, pp. 1–9.

Hoyt L (2011) *Crafting Nonfiction: Lessons on Writing Process, Traits and Craft.* Portsmouth, NH: Firsthand Heinemann.

Hudson J & Shapiro L (1991) From knowing to telling: The development of children's scripts, stories and personal narratives. In: McCabe A & Peterson C (eds) *Developing Narrative Structure*. New Jersey, Hove & London: Lawrence Erlbaum Associates.

Hughes M (1999) *Closing the Learning Gap.* Stafford: Network Educational Press.

Huitt W (2003) Conation as an important factor of mind. Available at: http://www.edpsyc interactive.org/topics/conation/conation.html

Hunt P (1999) *Understanding Children's Literature.* Abingdon: Routledge.

Hunt R (2003) *Biff's Aeroplane*: Oxford Reading Tree Stage 2: More Storybooks. Oxford: Oxford University Press.

Hyland K (2007) Genre pedagogy: Language, literacy and L2 writing instruction. *Journal of Second Language Writing* 16(3): 148–164.

Jasmine J & Weiner W (2007) The effects of writing workshop on abilities of first grade students to become confident and independent writers. *Early Childhood Education Journal* 35(2): 131–139.

Jewitt C, Bezemer J, Jones K & Kress G (2009) Changing English? The impact of technology and policy on a school subject in the 21st century. *English Teaching: Practice & Critique* 8(3): 8–20.

Jolliffe W (2004) *The National Literacy Strategy: Not Prescriptive Enough?* Paper presented at the British Educational Research Association Annual Conference, University of Manchester, (September) pp. 16–18.

Jones P (1988) *Lipservice: The Story of Talk in Schools.* Milton Keynes: Open University Press.

Katsarou E & Tsafos V (2010) Multimodality in L1 curriculum: The case of Greek compulsory education. *Critical Literacy: Theories & Practices* 4(1): 48–65.

Keen J (2010) Strategic revisions in the writing of Year 7 students in the UK. *The Curriculum Journal* 21(3): 255–280.

Keene EO & Zimmerman S (1997) *Mosaic of Thought: Teaching Comprehension in a Reader's Workshop.* Portsmouth, NH: Heinemann.

Kennedy E, Dunphy E, Dwyer B, Hayes G, McPhillips T, Marsh J, O'Connor M & Shiel G (2012) *Literacy in Early Childhood and Primary Education (3–8).* Commissioned research report for National Council for Curriculum and Assessment.

Kern D (2009) Cinderella's glass slipper and differentiating instruction. *The NERA Journal* 4(2): 83–94.

Kesner J & Matthews M (2003) Children learning with peers: The confluence of peer status and literacy competence within small-group literacy events. *Reading Research Quarterly* 38(2): 208–234.

King-Sears ME (2005) Scheduling for reading and writing small-group instruction using learning center designs. *Reading and Writing Quarterly* 21: 401–405.

Kingman Report (1998) *Committee of Enquiry into the Teaching of English Language.* London: HMSO.

Kirby P (1996) Teacher questions join storybook readings: Who's building whose building? *Reading* 30(1): 8–15.

Koki S (1998) Storytelling: The heart and soul of education. Available at: Pacific Resources for Education and Learning. Available at: http://www.prel.hawaii.edu

Korat O, Bahar E & Snapir M (2002) Sociodramatic play as opportunity for literacy development: The teacher's role. *The Reading Teacher* 56(4): 386–393.

Kress G (2003) *Literacy in the New Media Age.* London: Routledge.

Kress G (2010) *Multimodality: A Social Semiotic Approach to Contemporary Communication.* London: Routledge.

Kress G, Jewitt C, Ogborn J & Tsatarellis C (2001) Multimodal Teaching and Learning. London: Continuum Press.

Lambirth A & Goouch K (2006) Golden times of writing: the creative compliance of writing journals. *Literacy* 40(3): 146–152.

Makin L & Whiteman P (2006) Young children as active participants in the investigation of teaching and learning. *European Early Childhood Education Research Journal* 14(1): 33–41.

Mann C (2002) 1491. *Atlantic Monthly* 289(3): 41–53.

Marriott S (1991) *Picture Books in the Primary Classroom.* London: Paul Chapman Publishing.

Marriott S (1995) *Read On: Using Fiction in the Primary School.* London: Paul Chapman Publishing.

Marsh J & Millard E (2000) *Literacy and Popular Culture: Using Children's Culture in the Classroom.* London: Paul Chapman Publishing Limited.

Martin LE, Segraves R, Thacker S & Young L (2005) The writing process: Three first grade teachers and their students reflect on what was learned. *Reading Psychology* 26: 235–249.

Mason RA & Just MA (2011) Differentiable cortic networks for inferences concerning people's intentions versus physical causality. *Journal of Human Brain Mapping* 32: 313–329.

Matthews J (1999) *The Art of Childhood and Adolescence: The Construction of Meaning.* London: Falmer Press.

McAdamis S (2001) Teachers tailor their instruction to meet a variety of students' needs. *Journal of Staff Development* 22(2): 1–5.

McGee LM & Schickedanz JA (2007) Repeated interactive read-alouds in pre-school and kindergarten. *The Reading Teacher* 60(8): 742–751.

McKeown MG (2001) Text Talk: Capturing the benefits of read-aloud experiences for young children. *The Reading Teacher* 55(1): 10–20.

Meyer L, Wardrop J, Stahl S & Linn R (1994) Effects of reading storybooks aloud to children. *Journal of Educational Research* 88: 69–85.

Miller H (2002) Spelling: From invention to strategies. *Voices from the Middle* 9(3): 33–37.

Marsh J & Millard E (2001) Words with pictures: The role of visual literacy in writing and its implication for schooling. *Literacy* 35(2): 54–61.

Montgomery D (1997) *Spelling: Remedial Strategies.* London: Cassell.

Morris D & Templeton S (1999) Questions teachers ask about spelling. *Reading Research Quarterly* 34(1): 102–112.

Morris D & Templeton S (2000) Reconceptualizing spelling development and instruction. Available at: http://www.readingonline.org/articles/handbook/templeton/

Moustafa M & Dombey H (1998) *Whole to Part Phonics: How Children Learn to Read and Spell*. Centre for Language in Primary Education. Portsmouth, NH: Heinemann.

Moyles J & Worthington M (2011) *The Early Years Foundation Stage Through the Daily Experiences of Children*. Association for the Professional Development of Early Years Education: Occasional Paper No. 1, pp. 1–4.

Myhill D (2006) Talk, talk, talk: Teaching and learning in whole class discourse. *Research Papers in Education* 21(1): 19–41.

Myhill D & Locke T (2007) Composition in the English literacy classroom (editorial). *English Teaching: Practice and Critique* 6(1): 1–10.

National Curriculum Council (1989) *A Curriculum for All*. York: NNC.

National Writing Project (1985–1988).

New London Group (2000) A pedagogy of multiliteracies designing social futures. In: Cope B & Kalatzis M (eds) *Multiliteracies*. London: Routledge.

Nielsen C (2009) Children's embodied voices: Approaching children's experiences through multi-modal interviewing. *Phenomenology & Practice* 3(1): 80–93.

Nilsson M (2010) Developing voice in digital storytelling through creativity, narrative and multimodality. *International Journal of Media, Technology and Lifelong Learning* 6(2): 1–21.

Norris E & Kouider RC (1998) Children's use of drawing as a pre-writing strategy. *Journal of Research in Reading* 21(1): 69–74.

Norris E, Kouider M & Reichard C (2002) Children's use of drawing as a pre-writing strategy. *Journal of Research in Reading* 21(1): 69–74.

O'Brien A & Neal I (2007) Boys' writing: A 'hot topic'… but what are the strategies? *Education Today*. March: 1–15. Available at: http://www.education-today.net/obrien/boyswriting.pdf

Ogle DM (1986) K-W-L: A teaching model that develops active reading of expository text. *The Reading Teacher* (Feb) 6: 564–570.

Ohler J (2007) Digital storytelling in the classroom: New media pathways to literacy, learning and creativity. Thousand Oaks, CA: Corwin Press.

Olson R, Forsberg H & Wise B (1994) Genes, environment and the development of orthographic skills. In: Berninger VW (ed.) *The Varieties of Orthographic Knowledge II: Theoretical and Developmental Issues*. Dordrecht, The Netherlands: Kluwer Academic, pp. 21–71.

Oppel K (1903) Should children be told fairytales? A 1903 debate. *The History of Education and Childhood*. Available at: http://www.socsci.kun.nl/ped/whp/histeduc/disco1.html

Organisation for Economic Co-operation and Development (OECD) (2004) *OECD Thematic Review of Early Childhood Education and Care Policy in Ireland*. Dublin: The Stationery Office.

O'Sullivan O (2000) *Understanding Spelling*. London: CLPE.

Paris SG & Paris AH (2001) Classroom applications of research on self-regulated learning. *Educational Psychologist* 36(2): 89–101.

Patrick F, Forde C & McPhee A (2003) Challenging the 'new professionalism': From managerialism to pedagogy? *Journal of In-Service Education* 28(2): 237–253.

Pellegrini AD & Galda L (1991) Longitudinal relations among preschoolers symbolic play, metalinguistic verbs, and emergent literacy. In: Christie J (ed.), *Play and Early Literacy Development*. Albany: State University of New York Press. pp. 47–67.

Perrenoud P (1991) Towards a pragmatic approach to formative evaluation. In: Weston P (ed.) *Assessment of Pupils' Achievement: Motivation and School Success*. Amsterdam: Swets & Zeitlinger, pp. 79–101.

Perrenoud P (1998) From formative evaluation to a controlled regulation of learning pro-cesses: Towards a wider conceptual field. *Assessment in Education* 5(1): 85–102.

Perrone V (1994) Teaching for understanding: How to engage students in learning. *Educational Leadership* 51(5): 1–3.

Perry NE, Hutchinson L & Thauberger C (2007) Mentoring student teachers to design and implement literacy tasks that support self-regulated reading and writing. *Journal of Reading & Writing Quarterly* 23: 27–50.

Powell A (2001) Notes on the origins of meritocracy in American schooling. *History of Education Quarterly* 41(1): 73–80.

Pradl GM (1979) Learning how to begin and end a story. *Language Arts* 56: 21–25.

Pring R (2004) *Philosophy of Education*. London: Continuum.

Protheroe P (2010) *The Effect of Illustrations on the Ability of Children to Draw Inferences While Reading Narrative Texts*. Doctoral thesis submitted to the Victoria University of Wellington.

Purcell-Gates V, McIntyre E & Freppon PA (1995) Learning written storybook language in school: A comparison of low-SES children in skills-based and whole language class-rooms. *American Educational Research Journal* 32(3): 659–685.

Qualifications and Curriculum Authority (QCA) (2004) *More Than Words: Multimodal Texts in the Classroom*. London: QCA.

Read C (1975) *Children's Categorization of Speech in English*. Urbana, IL: National Council of Teachers of English.

Read C (1986) *Children's Creative Spelling*. London: Routledge & Kegan Paul.

Resnick LB & Williams Hall M (1998) Learning organisations for sustainable education reform. *Daedalus* Autumn: 1–6.

Resnick L (2000) *Learning Organisations for Sustainable Education Reform*. Keynote address to first ESRC Teaching and Learning Research Programme, University of Leicester.

Riggs EG (2004) Conation: Cultivating the *will* to succeed among middle and high school students. Forum on Public Policy. Available at: http://forumonpublicpolicy.com/archivesum07/riggs.pdf

Rijlaarsdam G, Braaksma M, Couzijn M, Janssen T, Raedts M, Van Steendam E, Toorenaar A & Van den Bergh H (2008) Observation of peers in learning to write: Practice and research. *Journal of Writing Research* 1(1): 53–83.

Robbins C & Ehri LC (1994) Reading storybooks to kindergartners helps them learn new vocabulary words. *Journal of Educational Psychology* 86(1): 54–64.

Roskos K & Christie J (2001) Examining the play-literacy interface: A critical review and future directions. *Journal of Early Childhood Literacy* 1(1): 59–89.

Ryokai K, Vaucelle C & Cassell J (2003) Virtual peers as partners in storytelling and literacy learning. *Journal of Computer Assisted Learning* 19(2): 195–208.

Sadler DR (1989) *Formative Assessment and the Design of Instructional Systems*. Boston, MA: Kluwer Academic Press.

Sadler DR (1998) Formative assessment: Revising the territory. *Assessment in Education* 5(1): 77–84.

Salvetti EP (2001) Project Story Boost: Read alouds for students at risk. *The Reading Teacher* 55(1): 76–83.

Santrock JW (2006) *Life-span Development*, 10th edn. New York: McGraw-Hill.

Saracho ON & Spodek B (2002) *Contemporary Perspectives in Literacy in Early Childhood Education*. Charlotte, NC: Information Age Publishing Inc.

Scardamalia M & Bereiter C (1986) Written composition. In: Wittrock MC (ed.) *Handbook of Research on Teaching*, 3rd edn. New York: Macmillan, pp. 778–803.

Schunk DH & Zimmerman BJ (1997) Social origins of self-regulatory competence. *Educational Psychologist* 32(4): 195–208.

Schunk DH & Zimmerman BJ (2007) Influencing children's self-efficacy and self-regulation of reading and writing through modelling. *Reading & Writing Quarterly* 23: 7–25.

Sénéchal M (2009) Literacy, language and emotional development. In: *Encyclopedia of Language and Literacy Development*. Canadian Language & Literacy Research Network, pp. 1–6.

Sénéchal M, Pagan S, Lever R & Ouellette GP (2008) Relations among the frequency of shared reading and 4-year-old children's vocabulary, morphological and syntax comprehension, and narrative skills. *Early Education and Development* 19(1): 27–44.

Shulman LS (1986) Those who understand: Knowledge growth in teaching. *Educational Researcher* 15(2): 4–14.

Shulman LS (1987) Knowledge and teaching: Foundations of the new reform. *Harvard Educational Review* 57(1): 1–22.

Silva ML, Abchi VS & Borzone A (2010) subordinated clauses usage and assessment of syntactic maturity: A comparison of oral and written retellings in beginning writers. *Journal of Writing Research* 2(1): 47–64.

Simmons V & Gebhardt A (2009) Concept of story. Available at: http://red6747.pbworks.com/Concept-of-Story

Sipe L (2001) Invention, convention and intervention: Invented spelling and the teacher's role. *The Reading Teacher* 55(3): 263–273.

Siraj-Blatchford I & Manni L (2008) 'Would you like to tidy up now?' An analysis of adult questioning in the Foundation Stage. *Early Years: An International Journal of Research and Development* 28(1): 5–22.

Smagorinsky P & O'Donnell-Allen C (2000) Idiocultural diversity in small groups: The role of the relational framework in collaborative learning. In: Lee CD & Smagorinsky P (eds) *Vygotskian Perspectives on Literary Research: Constructing Meaning Through Collaborative Inquiry*. New York: Cambridge University Press, pp. 165–190.

Smit D (1989) Some difficulties with collaborative learning. *Journal of Advanced Composition* 9(1/2): 45–58.

Smith L (1996) The social construction of rational understanding. In: Tryphon A & Vonege J (eds) *Piaget Vygotsky: The Social Genesis of Thought*. London: Psychology Press.

Stead T & Hoyt L (2012) *A Guide to Teaching Nonfiction Writing*. Portsmouth, NH: Firsthand Heinemann.

Steffler D, Varnhagen C, Friesen C & Trieman R (1998) There's more to children's spelling than the errors they make: Strategic and automatic processes for one-syllable words. *Journal of Educational Psychology* 90(3): 492–505.

Stuart M, Stainthorp R & Snowling M (2008) Literacy as a complex activity: Deconstructing the simple view of reading. *Literacy* 42(2): 59–66.

Sutherland R (2001) *Talk for writing*. Available at: http://jac.gsu.edu/jac/9/Aarticles/4.htm

Sykes EDA, Bell JF & Rodeiro CD (2009) *Birthdate Effects: A Review of the Literature from 1990-on*. Cambridge: Cambridge Assessment.

Tait-McCutcheon SL (2008) Self-efficacy in mathematics: Affective, cognitive and conative domains of functioning. In: Goos M, Brown R & Makar K (eds) *Proceedings of the 31st Annual Conference of the Mathematics Education Research Group of Australasia*.

Tatar M (1999) *The Classic Fairy Tales*. New York: W.W. Norton & Company.

Temple C, Nathan R, Temple F & Burris NA (1992) *The Beginnings of Writing*, 3rd edn. Needham Heights, MA: Pearson.

Templeton S & Morris D (1999) Reconceptualizing spelling development and instruction. In: Kamil ML, Mosenthal PB, Pearson PD & Barr R (eds) (2000) *Handbook of Reading Research*: Vol. 111. Mahwah, NJ: Erlbaum.

Tierney RJ & Shanahan T (1991) Research on the reading-writing relationship: Interactions, transactions, and outcomes. In: Barr R, Kamil ML, Mosenthal P, & Pearson PD (eds) *Handbook of Reading Research*: Vol. 2. New York: Longman. pp. 246–280.

Tizard B, Hughes M, Carmichael H & Pinkerton G (1983) Language and social class: Is verbal deprivation a myth? *Journal of Child Psychology* 24(4): 533–542.

Tomlinson CA (2001) Differentiated instruction in the regular classroom: What does it mean? How does it look? *Understanding Our Gifted* 14(1): 3–6.

Topping K (2001) *Thinking, Reading, Writing: A Practical Guide to Paired Learning with Peers, Parents and Volunteers*. London and New York: Continuum.

Treiman R (1993) *Beginning to Spell: A Study of First-grade Children*. New York, NY: Oxford University.

Troia GA & Graham S (2003) Effective writing instruction across the grades: What every educational consultant should know. *Journal of Educational and Psychological Consultation* 14(1): 75–89.

US Department of Education (2008) *Accessing Skills Towards Successful Writing Development*. US Department of Education, Office of Special Education Programs: Washington DC.

Vanderburg RM (2006) Reviewing research on teaching writing based on Vygotsky's theories: What we can learn. *Reading & Writing Quarterly* 22(4): 375–393.

Vandergrift KE (1995) On sharing literature with young people. Available at: http://comminfo. rutgers.edu/professional-development/childlit/sharelit.html

Varnhagen C, Boechler PM & Steffler DJ (1999) Phonological and orthographic influences on children's vowel spelling. *Scientific Studies of Reading* 3: 363–379.

Vorvilas G, Karalis T & Ravanis K (2010) Applying multimodal discourse analysis to learning objects' user interface. *Contemporary Educational Technology* 1(3): 255–266.

Voss RF (1983) Composition and the empirical imperative. *Journal of Advanced Composition* 4: 5–12.

Vygotsky LS (1962) *Thought and Language*. Cambridge, MA: MIT Press.

Vygotsky L (1978) *Mind in Society: The Development of Higher Psychological Processes* (trans). Cambridge, MA: Harvard University Press.

Waddell M & Benson P (1992) *Owl Babies*. London: Walker Books.

Wells G (2001a) *Action, Talk and Text: Learning and Teaching through Inquiry*. New York: Teachers College Press.

Wells G (2001b) The case for dialogic inquiry. In: Wells G (ed.) *Action, Talk and Text: Learning and Teaching through Inquiry*. New York: Teachers College Press.

Weston P (1992) A decade for differentiation. *British Journal of Special Education* 19(1): 6–9.

Whitehead M (1997) *Language and Literacy in the Early Years*. London: Paul Chapman.

Whitehurst GJ, Crone DA, Zevnbergen AA, Shultz MD, Velting ON & Fischel JE (1999) Outcomes of an emergent literacy intervention from Head Start through to second grade. *Journal of Educational Psychology* 91(2): 261–272.

Wilde S (1992) *You Kan Red this! Spelling and Punctuation for Whole Language Classrooms, K-6*. Portsmouth, NH: Heinemann.

Wilford S (2000) From play to literacy: Implications for the classroom. Available at: http:// ecap.crc.illinois.edu/pubs/katzsym/wilford.html

Williams P (2008) *Independent Review of Mathematics Teaching in Early Years Settings and Primary Schools: Final Report*. Nottingham: DCSF.

Williams TL (2007) 'Reading' the painting: Exploring visual literacy in the primary grades. *The Reading Teacher* 60(7): 636–642.

Wiseman A (2003) Collaboration, initiation and rejection: The social construction of stories in a kindergarten class. *The Reading Teacher* 56(8): 802–810.

Wong YY (2002) Responding to Rebecca Howard's essay on collaborative pedagogy. Available at: http://english.ohio-state.edu/wong.236/critical-responses.html

Wood K, Roser N & Martinez M (2001) Collaborative literacy: Lessons learned from literature. *The Reading Teacher* 55(2): 102–111.

Wray D & Lewis M (1996) An approach to writing non-fiction. *Reading* July: 7–13.

Wray D & Lewis M (2000) Developing non-fiction writing: beyond writing frames. In Evans J (ed.) *The Writing Classroom*. London: David Fulton. pp. 108–115.

Wyse D, McCreery E & Torrance H (2007) *The Trajectory and Impact of National Reform: Curriculum and Assessment in English Primary Schools: Primary Review Interim Report*. Cambridge: University of Cambridge, Faculty of Education.

Yaden D, Rowe D & MacGillivay L (1999) *Emergent Literacy: A Polyphony of Perspectives*. University of Michigan School of Education, Ann Arbor, MI: CIERA.

Yarrow F & Topping KJ (2001) Collaborative writing: the effect of metacognitive prompting and structured peer interaction. *British Journal of Educational Psychology* 71(2): 261–282.

Yopp HK & Yopp RH (2000) Supporting phonemic awareness development in the classroom. *The Reading Teacher* 54(2): 130–143.

Zhoa Y (2003) Constructing social and academic identities through talk as part of the composing process. Available at: http://www.tigersystm.net/aera2003/reviewproposal.text

Zimmerman BJ (2000) Attaining self-regulation: A social-cognitive perspective. In: Boekarts M, Pintich PR & Zeidner M (eds) *Handbook of Self-regulation*. San Diego: Academic Press, pp. 13–39.

Zitlow CS (2000) Sounds and pictures in words: Images in literature for young adults. Available at: http://scholar.lib.vt.edu/ejournals/ALAN/winter00/zitlow.html

INDEX